"Dr. Kenneth Bailey's unique perspective as one who has spent the better part of his life living in the Middle East unlocks the parables and teachings of our Lord Jesus in remarkably fresh ways. In the unfolding of the prodigal son Bailey demonstrates there is no forgiveness without great cost on the part of the forgiver. This revised edition is a wonderful update and expansion of an already excellent book. I am delighted to commend it."

THE RIGHT REV. JOHN W. HOWE, D.D., BISHOP, EPISCOPAL CHURCH DIOCESE OF CENTRAL FLORIDA

"*The Cross & the Prodigal* is a little book that changed the minds of Gospel scholars throughout the world. In its original edition (1973) Bailey not only established himself as a leading New Testament interpreter, but he launched an approach to the Gospels that was utterly unique. Over sixty years of life in the Middle East (from Egypt to Iraq) bequeathed to him a discerning knowledge of peasant life; fluency in Arabic; the ability to work in Syriac, Coptic and Aramaic; and an intimate acquaintance with Rabbinic literature. These skills he now applies to the three parables of Luke 15 in order to unlock Middle Eastern New Testament studies—and today Bailey's legacy belongs with scholars such as Joachim Jeremias: leading parable interpreters whose work has been a watershed for the rest of us."

GARY M. BURGE, PH.D., PROFESSOR OF NEW TESTAMENT, WHEATON COLLEGE AND GRADUATE SCHOOL

"This book is for those of us who long to know what Jesus was saying to his audience then, so that we can know what the Bible is saying to us now. Ken Bailey's work is very nourishing, spiritually and theologically. And if you like to be surprised with new insights, you will love *The Cross & the Prodigal!*"

THE REV. MARIAN McCLURE, PH.D., DIRECTOR, WORLDWIDE MINISTRIES, PRESBYTERIAN CHURCH (U.S.A.)

"It is an extremely rare event in New Testament studies when the historical expertise of the scholar is combined with the poetic imagination of the storyteller. Ken Bailey's *The Cross & the Prodigal* unites the professor and the playwright. In the first section of the book the author's unique familiarity with Christian literature of Near Eastern provenance and his intimate knowledge of Near Easter village life produce a fascinating explanation of the parable of the prodigal son, which emerges not as the sentimental account of the pilgrimage of a sorry sinner, but as the portrayal of God as a Father who pays every price possible in the search of two lost sons, a portrait contrary to all expectations associated with a patriarch. The book's second section is a play in four scenes in which this understanding of the parable is placed on the stage. Thus, exegetical theology is transformed back into its original medium, the telling of a story."

ULRICH MAUSER, OTTO A. PIPER PROFESSOR OF BIBLICAL THEOLOGY EMERITUS, PRINCETON THEOLOGICAL SEMINARY

"In *The Cross & the Prodigal* Kenneth Bailey uses his rare and intimate familiarity with the peasant culture of the Middle East to illuminate three beloved parables: the lost sheep, the lost coin and the lost son. Bailey rightly believes that Christian communities with close connections to the biblical world have many things to teach us about the cultural background of biblical narrative. This classic work, newly revised, provides fresh perspectives for understanding the love of God the Father, and for seeing how the compassion of the cross is present already in the teaching ministry of Jesus Christ."

PHILIP GRAHAM RYKEN, SENIOR MINISTER, TENTH PRESBYTERIAN CHURCH, PHILADELPHIA

The Cross & the Prodigal

Luke 15 Through the Eyes of
Middle Eastern Peasants

KENNETH E. BAILEY

IVP Books

An imprint of InterVarsity Press
Downers Grove, Illinois

InterVarsity Press
P.O. Box 1400, Downers Grove, IL 60515-1426
World Wide Web: www.ivpress.com
E-mail: email@ivpress.com

Second Edition ©2005 by Kenneth E. Bailey. First Edition ©1973 Concordia Publishing House, St Louis, Missouri, USA

InterVarsity Press® is the book-publishing division of InterVarsity Christian Fellowship/USA®, a student movement active on campus at hundreds of universities, colleges and schools of nursing in the United States of America, and a member movement of the International Fellowship of Evangelical Students. For information about local and regional activities, write Public Relations Dept., InterVarsity Christian Fellowship/USA, 6400 Schroeder Rd., P.O. Box 7895, Madison, WI 53707-7895, or visit the IVCF website at <www.intervarsity.org>.

Design: Cindy Kiple
Images: prodigal son: Erich Lessing/Art Resource, NY
   wooden compartments and borders: Arab Art as Seen Through the Monuments of Cairo from the 7th Century to the End of the 18th Century

ISBN 978-0-8308-3281-1

Printed in the United States of America ∞

Library of Congress Cataloging-in-Publication Data

Bailey, Kenneth E.
 The Cross & the prodigal: Luke 15 through the eyes of Middle
 Eastern peasants/Kenneth E. Bailey.—2nd ed.
  p. cm.
 Includes bibliographical references.
 ISBN 0-8308-3281-5 (pbk.: alk. paper)
 1. Prodigal son (Parable) 2. Bible. N.T. Luke XV—Commentaries. 3.
 Prodigal son (Parable)—Drama. 4. Bible plays, American. I. Title:
 Cross and the prodigal. II. Title.
 BT378.P8B24 2005
 226.8'06—dc22

               2005004484

P	19	18	17	16	15	14	13	12	11	10	9	8	7	6	5	4	3	2
Y	22	21	20	19	18	17	16	15	14	13	12	11	10	09	08	07			

To

Ustaz Nageeb Ibraheem

in whose heart shines the light

which the night cannot overcome,

and the light of whose life has guided me

through much darkness

Contents

Introduction to the
Second Edition

I t is almost forty years since I wrote this little book, and it is with joy and much gratitude that I see it reappearing. The editors of InterVarsity Press have invited me to reflect briefly on the journey that the work inaugurated. I count it a privilege to do so.

Andrew Walls, the renowned Scottish historian of non-Western Christianity, has affirmed on numerous occasions that the modern missionary movement launched new academic disciplines. He mentions anthropology and linguistics, along with Asian and African studies. Perhaps there is another discipline that needs to be added to such a distinguished list: Middle Eastern New Testament studies. For many, this proposed field may sound like a contradiction in terms. Isn't the Middle East the heartland of Islam? What does that world have to do with the New Testament? Is there any data for Middle Eastern New Testament studies?

There are more Arabic-speaking Christians in the Middle East than Jews in the entire world. This demographic fact is generally unknown in the West, where all Arabs are often assumed to be Muslims. The result is that even though there were Arabic speakers present on Pentecost (Acts 2:11), millions of Arab Christians today are almost invisible to the Western world. There are at least three plausible reasons for this reality.

Shortly after World War II, Winston Churchill described the critical divide that had occurred between Eastern and Western Europe as an "Iron Curtain." In the early Christian centuries, not one but three curtains fell across the Mediterranean basin separating the Middle East from Europe.

The first of these was the Council of Chalcedon (A.D. 451), which resulted in a deep split between the churches of the Greek and Roman worlds on the one hand, and most of the churches of the Eastern Mediterranean on the other. A second curtain fell with the Islamic invasions of the early seventh century. As Islam poured across the Middle East and swept North Africa, Spain and, in time, also Asia Minor and the Balkans, there was a great divide between "the Christian world" and "the Islamic world." Sadly, Eastern Christians, overrun by powerful Muslim forces, were largely forgotten. A third curtain can be called the linguistic curtain. The primary languages of non-Chalcedonian Eastern Christians have historically been Syriac, Coptic and Arabic. These difficult tongues are rarely learned by New Testament scholars. The result of these three curtains is that Eastern Christianity, with all of its spiritual treasures, remains largely unknown. This means that for roughly 1,500 years we in the West have been interpreting the New Testament with virtually no contact with the Christians of the Eastern Mediterranean who, in a unique way, are inheritors of the traditional culture of the Middle East and thereby the culture of the Bible.

As a Jew, Jesus participated in Middle Eastern culture and its milieu. Yes, Hellenism was a powerful force in Jesus' day, but his primary languages were Aramaic and Hebrew—not Greek. What difference does all of this make to my exegetical journey through Luke 15 and Middle Eastern culture that this little book begins to document?

My forty-year sojourn among Middle Eastern Christians was in its formative early years when I wrote *The Cross and the Prodigal*. Throughout those decades I was working, thinking and teaching in Arabic and thus participating in church life as I studied and taught Semitic-based Gospels to predominantly Semitic peoples. Those years ingrained a very deep awareness in me.

If theology is expressed in concepts and structured by philosophy and logic, the primary tools required are a good mind and the ability to think logically. But if theology is presented in story form, the meaning of the story cannot be fairly ascertained without becoming, as much as possible, a part of the culture of the storyteller and his or her listeners. A wonderful illustration of this dilemma is set forth by N. T. Wright in his new book on the Resurrection.[1] Wright borrows an illustration from George Caird who records the sentence, "I am mad about my flat." In the mouth of an American this

---

[1]N. T. Wright, *The Resurrection of the Son of God* (Minneapolis: Fortress, 2003).

means, "I am angry because someone has punctured one of the tires on my car." But for the British the same statement means, "I am very excited about my new living quarters." The culture of the speaker must be penetrated if what is said is to be understood. Even so with the life and teachings of Jesus. The Spirit has not been without a witness across the centuries. Yet there are layers of perception that can only be uncovered when the culture of the Middle East is understood and applied to the interpretation of Scripture. Luke 15 is a primary example of this truth.

Is it shameful for a young man to ask for his inheritance when his father is still alive? Is it ominous when his older brother remains silent? How is the father expected to respond? Does the youth shame his family in the community by selling his portion of the property? When the son "came to himself" was he "repenting" or "trying to get something to eat?" Why is there no mother in the story? Does the father humiliate himself by running down the road? Can a father leave his guests to go out and talk to an older son who is pouting in the courtyard? If he does, what does it mean? These and many other questions gradually appeared on the screen of my mind as I was privileged to live and learn in the Middle East from my youth through nearly three score years and ten.

This book was my first attempt at taking Middle Eastern culture as a starting point for interpretation of a well-known passage of the Gospels. Granted, no one can simplistically assume that the contemporary Middle East is identical to the first century. But in its conservative traditional villages, the Middle East provided a cultural place to stand where the above questions forced themselves on me and cried out for thoughtful answers. Without that place to stand the questions themselves would not have occurred to me, and consequently I would not have sought their answers. Regardless of its limitation, it was clear to me that Middle Eastern culture was a better lens through which to examine the parables of Jesus than my inherited contemporary American culture.

My study of Luke 15 has evolved in both method and perception. I am conscious of five distinct stages:

1. Traditional Middle Eastern culture. My starting point was the above mentioned privilege of living among and learning from Middle Eastern Christians.

2. Eastern Christian New Testament literature. Early in my study and research I slowly became aware of 1,800 years of translations of the text of the New Testament from Greek into Syriac and Coptic and then into Arabic.

Translation always involves interpretation. Every translation is a minicommentary. The earliest of these translations have been my daily companion for decades. I then discovered the great Syriac commentators on the New Testament, such as Hibatallah ibn al-Assal and Abdallah ibn al-Tayyib. These and other Arabic language scholars remain largely unpublished in any language and thereby unknown beyond a narrow circle in the Middle East. Tens of thousands of exegetical sermons in manuscript form await me.

3. Rabbinics. There is no substitute for original sources. Reading the Mishnah from cover to cover twice was an exciting adventure, partially because as I read I found myself back in the kind of traditional Middle Eastern village of the type I had already experienced. The sense of déjà vu was strong indeed as I read. After that formative exposure to Judaica I could see clearly that the primary structures of daily life, which I had already observed in conservative Middle Eastern village life, could be documented from the sayings of first- and second-century rabbis from Babylon to Jerusalem. Reading most of the twenty-nine volumes of the Babylonian Talmud provided important additional data, as did the Jerusalem Talmud. Living for some years in the world of the ten volumes of the Midrash Rabbah was also rewarding, not to mention the Tosefta and the Targumim.

The issue is not the economic, political and societal changes that are inevitable in any community. Nor do I assume that a third-century rabbinic interpretation of a particular Psalm was necessarily current in the first century. Rather, as I have already written elsewhere,

> to interpret the parables of Jesus, the interpreter (consciously or unconsciously) will inevitably make decisions about attitudes toward women, men, the family, the family structure, family loyalties and their requirements, children, architectural styles, agricultural methods, leaders, scholars, religious authorities, trades, craftsmen, servants, eating habits, money, loyalty to community, styles of humor, story-telling, methods of communication, use of metaphor, forms of argumentation, forms of reconciliation, attitudes toward time, toward governmental authorities, what shocks and at what level, reactions to social situations, reasons for anger, attitudes toward animals, emotional and cultural reactions to various colors, dress, sexual codes, the nature of personal and community honor and its importance, and many, many other things.[2]

Every human being, regardless of his or her culture, has a set of attitudes that shape all of the above. These culturally conditioned attitudes function unconsciously and inevitably influence the way any person reads any story. It is my Middle Eastern experience of these things, confirmed through a serious reading of early rabbinic sources, that has provided me with an escape hatch from my own Western cultural imprisonment.

4. *Psalm 23.* As my journey through the mind of Jesus the rabbi continued, I gradually came to see that the parable of the lost sheep in Luke 15:3-7 was a "rewrite" of the beloved Shepherd's psalm. Following this lead, I discovered many new treasures in the parable.[3]

5. *Jacob.* At times one stumbles onto a new discovery when not looking for it. Such was the case when I listened to a very astute lecture on the story of Jacob during which the penny dropped. Stimulated by that lecture, I gradually became aware of fifty-one points of comparison and contrast between the story of Jacob in Genesis 27:1—36:8 and the parable of the prodigal son. In constructing the great parable of the two lost sons, Jesus was clearly rewriting the primary story that gave Israel its name and its identity.[4]

Another aspect of the importance of this great parable is the subject of Christian witness to or dialogue/confrontation with Islam. September 11, 2001, and its aftermath have brought Christianity and Islam face to face in far more critical ways today than was the case forty years ago. Islam continues to read the parable of the prodigal son as a denial of both the incarnation and the atonement. (On the surface it appears that the prodigal is reconciled to his father by his own unaided efforts. If so, Jesus reflects Islamic theology in this parable.) The *Cross and the Prodigal* tries to bring some answers to this challenge.

For me, a decades-long journey began with this book. Is it a "voice crying in the wilderness"? Perhaps. I hope not. Will other voices, more able than mine, appear that can plumb more deeply the Eastern cultural world and more precisely interpret the inexhaustible richness of stories from and about Jesus? I earnestly hope so. Is this cautious, unsteady step a possible beginning to a new discipline that might one day be christened "Middle Eastern New Testament Studies"? I don't know. All I can do is hope that once again

---

[2]Kenneth E. Bailey, *Finding the Lost: Cultural Keys to Luke 15* (St. Louis: Concordia, 1992), p. 32.
[3]This led to the writing of *Finding the Lost.*
[4]See Kenneth E. Bailey, *Jacob and the Prodigal: How Jesus Retold Israel's Story* (Downers Grove, Ill.: InterVarsity Press, 2003).

your young men shall see visions,
and your old men shall dream dreams. (Joel 2:28; Acts 2:17)

A final word is perhaps in order regarding the drama that is part of this work. If "story" is a serious mode of theological language that effectively creates meaning, then emotion and drama cannot be ignored. The difficulty is that contemporary "biblical drama" often overlaps with fiction, and in the process the fiction overwhelms the biblical text and its message. As this happens drama becomes a deliberately crafted tool for presenting the ideas of the dramatist in violation of the vision of the biblical author.

I have written the scripts for two professionally produced feature-length films; one of which is based on the three parables of Luke 15.[5] In the year-long process of script revision for the latter and during the filming itself, I found myself under constant pressure to ignore the perceived ideas of Jesus and allow the drama to present the ideas of the film director. With the backing of the film's producers this leverage was successfully resisted, but it was always there. Perhaps such pressures have historically helped keep serious biblical interpretation and biblical drama apart. In addition, it may not have occurred to many that a good story engages the emotions and that drama can be disciplined to serve the purposes of serious exegesis.

It is my hope that others will be inspired to venture down this often neglected path. From the first I was determined to unite serious exegesis and serious drama. They belong together. The reader will be the judge of the success or failure of this wedding.

Yes, "a journey of a thousand miles begins with one step." A corollary to that famous phrase is "the first step must be in the right direction." Looking back I sense that the "first step" made by this modest effort was in the right direction.

My prayer, gentle reader, is that these three parables of Jesus, here clarified, may encourage you in your journey of faith even as they have encouraged me in mine.

"He was dead and is alive.
He was lost and is found."

Kenneth E. Bailey

---

[5] *He Was Lost and Is Found,* a film produced in Cairo, Egypt, is in Arabic (with English subtitles). 110 minutes.

Preface

Across the centuries since the rise of Islam, Muslim voices have echoed the cry "Christians have perverted the message of Jesus" and pointed to the famous parable of the prodigal son as evidence. Their case can be stated as follows:

> In this parable the Father obviously represents God while the younger son represents humankind. The son leaves home, gets into trouble and finally decides to return to his Father. He *"yistaghfir Allah"* (he seeks the forgiveness of God). On arrival the Father welcomes the son and thus demonstrates that he, the father, is *"rahman wa rahim"* (merciful and compassionate). There is no cross and no incarnation, no "son of God" and no "savior," no "word that becomes flesh" and no "way of salvation," no death and no resurrection, no mediator and no mediation. The son needs no help to return home. The result is obvious. Jesus is a good Muslim who in this parable affirms Muslim theology. The heart of the Christian faith is thus denied by the very prophet Christianity claims to follow. Islam with neither a cross nor a savior preserves the true message of the prophet Jesus.

Arab Christians in the Middle East have grappled with this crisis of interpretation for more than a millennium. In various forms the modern world now faces the same crisis. As a result of emigration and a series of international conflicts, the interface between Christianity and Islam is upon us, ready or not! What can be said about this reality?

R. C. Trench in his famous *Notes on the Parables of Our Lord* observes that for centuries the story of the prodigal son has been called *Evangelium in*

Evangelio (the gospel in the Gospel). Trench affirms that this title is abundantly justified.[1] If across the centuries this is the way the church has seen this parable, how is it that both the incarnation (God comes to us in Jesus) and the atonement (the cross is a saving power) appear to be missing? If the cross is essential for forgiveness, why does it seem to be absent in this parable? Having spent four decades serving the Arab Christian churches of the Middle East, these and other related theological questions have required answers of me. A part of this book is a summary of the answers I have found to the above challenge.

I have discussed the three parables of the lost sheep, the lost coin and the two lost sons (the prodigal son) extensively with scholars, pastors, elders, and illiterate farmers across the Arab world, and I have struggled to understand it in its Middle Eastern cultural setting. In addition I have followed the centuries-old commentaries on the Gospel of Luke written in Arabic and Syriac, along with the commentaries on these parables in the Western tradition. The relevant early literature of the Jewish community in the Mishnah and the two Talmuds have been scrutinized as well. Half a century of study has produced for me a series of new insights as I tried to see these parables through Middle Eastern eyes.

The result has been a new way to talk about the heart of our faith that can speak to the Muslim mind of the East and hopefully to the secular mindset of the West. It is my prayer that it may also be of use in explaining the Christian faith in the global South.

For years music has aided immeasurably in communicating the emotional content of the Psalms. Part two of this book is a drama that seeks to express the theological and the emotional content of this parable. The play *Two Sons Have I Not* is written both to be read (privately or publicly) and acted. For centuries dramatists have taken biblical stories and shaped them to describe their own ideas, often deliberately ignoring the intent of the biblical authors. This is not my goal. Rather, this play tries to present, in dramatic form, theological content that I am convinced is placed in the story by its original composer, Jesus of Nazareth. Those who shared his culture would have had these ideas available to them directly in the parable itself. For people of other times and cultures the drama hopefully can help clarify and communicate that same meaning along with the dramatic

---

[1]R. C. Trench, *Notes on the Parables of our Lord* (London: John W. Parker, 1857), p. 387.

tensions and the emotions that are at the heart of the story.

Jesus spoke to a Middle Eastern peasant people. Even the educated would have had their roots in that peasantry. What lies between the lines, what is felt and not spoken, is of deepest significance. Indeed, it almost cannot be expressed because it is not consciously apprehended. What "everybody knows" is never explained.

In the Middle East "everybody knows" that to be polite to your father is much more important than to obey him. Jesus disagrees. So he tells a story of a father and his two boys in which he declares that the good son is the son who obeyed, even if he was rude to his father (Matthew 21:28-32). When we do not know the underlying village attitudes, it is easy to miss the revolutionary nature of the parable.

The Middle Eastern peasantry has survived through the ages almost unchanged. In isolated villages, I have found young girls making clay dolls that look much like the fertility goddesses of Old Testament times. Patterns of speech, dress and family structure remain stubbornly the same. Father Henry Ayrout, in his famous anthropological monograph on the Egyptian peasant titled *The Fellaheen*, writes:

> The fellaheen have changed their masters, their religion, their language, and their crops, but not their manner of life. . . . [V]iolent and repeated shocks have swept away whole peoples, as can be seen today from the ruins of North Africa or Chaldea, . . . but the fellaheen have held firm and stood their ground. . . . They are as impervious and enduring as the granite of their temples and as slow to develop. . . . This is not merely an impression. We can see the fellah using the same implements—the plough, the shaduf, the saqia, . . . the same methods of treating the body, . . . many of the same marriage and funeral customs. Through the pages of Herodotus, Diodorus Siculus, Strabo, Maqrizi, Vansleb, Pere Sicard and Volney, we can recognize the same fellah. No revolution, no evolution.[2]

Almost everyone, ancient or modern, who has had the privilege of working over an extended period in villages of the Mideast testifies to the same fact: the granitelike conservatism of the peasantry. Today one of the highest compliments one villager can give to his fellow is the title "Preserver of the

---

[2]Henry Habib Ayrout, *The Fellaheen*, trans. Hilary Wayment, rev. ed. (Cairo: R. Schindler, 1945), pp. 19-20.

Customs." As a result, in the main, village attitudes are of great antiquity.

When a Japanese Christian artist paints a portrait of the Madonna and child, the figures look Japanese. If one would insist on literalism, the figures are "distorted" by community and culture. Still the picture communicates something essential and meaningful. Indeed, the Japanese distinctives are what give the painting its significance. Western understandings of the Scriptures are likewise conditioned by Western history and culture. There is no escape. I cannot push the bus on which I am riding. No one, in any culture, is a disembodied eye looking down on the world from outer space. If then a cultural "coloring" is inevitable, why not seek it in a peasant society as close to first-century Palestine as possible? The only alternative for all of us who hail from outside of the Middle East is to fall back on our own cultural perceptions. The only eyes I have through which I can view the world are my own. It is the basic presupposition of this study that the insights gained from looking at the parable of the prodigal son through the eyes of conservative Middle Eastern peasant society (ancient and modern) are a better starting point than the cultures of North America or Europe.

In this study, volumes of traditional material, critical and expository, have been omitted. Nor have I tried to interact with the various contemporary commentators on these parables. The emphasis of this book is on new insights.

Jesus spoke Aramaic, Hebrew and certainly some Greek. Whether Luke's sources for the parables were Greek or Aramaic, written or oral, I will not try to debate here. Yet at a few points I will refer to the twelve-hundred-year-old Arabic Bible tradition that is a lake into which interpretive streams from Coptic, Greek and Syriac have flowed. This Arabic translation tradition is almost unheard of and thereby unexamined.

Across the twentieth century in biblical studies, forms of speech were taken very seriously. Here again village speech forms are also enlightening and will be referred to when appropriate.

All biblical quotations are from the Revised Standard Version or from my own translations of the original Greek.

Arabic calligraphy has been an art form in the Middle East for over a thousand years. Islam forbids the use of any human or animal form in religious art. Decorative writing often fills the gap created thereby. Muslim artists only beautify the text. In the plates that introduce the chapters I have tried to take this art form one step further by attempting to represent symbolically something of the text's meaning. Each plate has its accompanying translation and commentary.

Wherever possible I have made the language inclusive but occasionally have used *he* for *he and she* when the latter is awkward in sentence construction. This is for clarity only and no disrespect to any reader is intended.

My thanks goes out to Mr. Andrew Le Peau of InterVarsity Press who has given me the opportunity to completely rewrite this material for this new edition. I am profoundly grateful to Miss Elizabeth Hill, who during two successive Egyptian summers, in the midst of unbearable heat, typed the first two drafts of the first edition of this manuscript. She patiently endured my handwriting and corrected my abominable spelling. I am also indebted to Mrs. Evelyn Steele of Pittsburgh, who in spite of many family responsibilities graciously volunteered to type the third revision, which was equally illegible.

Sara Bailey has painstakingly corrected and revised the entire text of this new edition and to her I am deeply grateful. Inexpressible thanks to my dear wife, without whose partnership in life this manuscript could never have been written.

Soli Deo Gloria!

The decorative Arabic calligraphy below the title of part one says, "And he said, 'A certain man had two sons.'" The characters on the right symbolize the younger son, who stands outside his father's fellowship in rebellion.

The older son (the characters on the left) seems to have a tenuous hold within the house, but in reality he too stands outside.

Both sons are equally present from the first.

Commentary on Luke 15

CHAPTER ONE

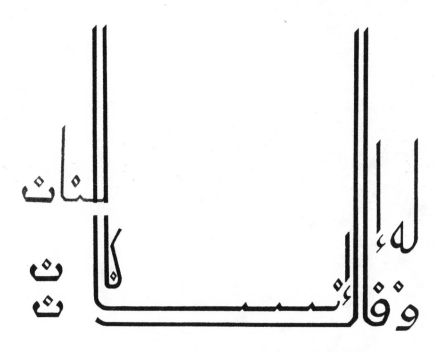

Rejoice with Me

In Luke's Gospel, Jesus begins his final journey to Jerusalem in chapter 9 and arrives in chapter 19. In that section the simmering conflict with the Pharisees comes to a head with their ominous complaint, "This man receives sinners." In this plate their words (appearing on the bottom of the text) reveal their inner selves. With the addition of two brief strokes, the towering heavy lines appear as pillars in a building because the Pharisees see themselves as the pillars of the house of Israel. The outer lines are strong and foreboding.

In the midst of their complaint is the shepherd's happy cry, "Rejoice with me!" Jesus, via the shepherd, calls on the Pharisees to fill their hearts with the joy of welcoming a returning sinner into their fellowship. The shepherd's cry is open, free and joyous.

هذ إقبل خطاة إفرحوا معي

Rejoice with Me
This Man Receives Sinners

1

Rejoice with Me

LUKE 15:1-10

*Now the tax collectors and sinners were all
drawing near to hear him. And the Pharisees and the
scribes murmured, saying, "This man receives sinners
and eats with them." So he told them this parable. (Verses 1-3)*

Violent storms arise quickly on the Sea of Galilee. Even seasoned sailors such
as Peter and John were sometimes caught in them. Luke 15 begins with rumblings more ominous than thunder over the lake. The religious establishment
felt threatened by the innovator in their midst. When he told these stories,
Jesus was himself on the way to Jerusalem, where the storm would break on
him in an attempt to eliminate the threat he posed to the ruling elite.[1]

The three deceptively simple stories in Luke 15 build toward a tense climax in the confrontation between the father and the older son at the end of
the parable of the prodigal son.[2] What will the older son do with the plea
for reconciliation offered to him at great cost? When the conflict of the drama
reaches this unbearable pitch, the curtain falls without a conclusion. All of
this is evident only when we keep in mind the audience and the issue that
brought the Pharisees to Jesus with their grumbling.

---

[1] Luke 9:51 reads: "When the days drew near for him to be received up, he set his face to go
to Jerusalem." There follows a large block of teaching material that has been called "The Travel
Document." Luke 15 is well into the middle of this material. Thus these parables must be understood in the light of the fact that Christ has already set his face to go to Jerusalem.
[2] Luke 15 has long been considered a unit by many scholars. We will proceed with this as a
basic assumption.

The audience to whom Jesus spoke was composed of Pharisees and scribes, the "righteous" of the community. Their complaint was that "this man receives sinners and eats with them." Three parties were involved: the religious (the Pharisees), the irreligious (sinners) and Jesus. All three of these parties (the "found," the "lost" and Jesus) appear in each of the three parables. Yet there is a noticeable progression to the accounts. The first story deals with animals. The second is about lifeless coins. But in the third story people walk on the stage and begin talking.

During the time of Jesus, tax collectors were naturally seen as "sinners." When any ethnic community is forcibly incorporated into someone else's empire, tax collectors are inevitably despised intensely. But the Roman Empire presented a special problem. It collected taxes through "tax farmers." An individual would buy from the rulers the right to collect taxes in a certain area. That person was then able for the most part to set his own rates and exact whatever he could. He was bound by contract to deliver a certain sum to the authorities. The rest was his. These "tax farmers" were often Gentiles. In Palestine local people were then hired to do the actual collecting of the money.[3] Obviously, with unscrupulous men involved, there was a great deal of graft.

The practice still persists at one point in modern Egyptian village life where a local citizen contracts from the government the right to tax the use of the village riverbank crossing on the Nile. He then hires men to collect a premium from every person who crosses the river. The going rate is whatever the traffic will bear. Graft and favoritism become the rule when unscrupulous men seize control of the village crossing point. The last years of the Turkish Empire saw the same ancient system at work, and once again widespread abuse was common.

Furthermore, Palestine in the first century was occupied by imperialists. It is difficult for anyone who has never lived in an occupied country to fully appreciate the hatred generated toward the "collaborator." (Modern African and Asian nationalisms give us many parallels.) In modern Arab politics the bitterest of all insults is "agent of the imperialists."

When a colony approaches the ignition point of revolt, it hates any "collaborator" with ferocious intensity. Suddenly the collaborators' compromises with national honor become unendurable. In Jesus' day nationalistic

---

[3]John R. Donahue, "Tax Collector," *Anchor Bible Dictionary,* ed. David Noel Freedman (New York: Doubleday, 1992), 6:337-38.

forces in Judea and Galilee were gathering strength. The smoldering of revolt would burst into flame within a few years. Any cooperation with Rome and its tax collectors was surely looked on as a betrayal of race and religion.

In the Gospels the title of tax collector is usually linked with *sinners* or with *adulterers* and quite naturally with *Gentiles*.[4] The most common identification is with *sinners*. In the mouth of a Pharisee *sinners* meant the "unclean," the "breakers of the Law" and those of low moral character generally. In short, anyone they condemned. Luke uses *sinner* thirteen times and generally means by it people of low moral character. Here he is quoting the Pharisees, and thus the added flavor of "traitor" and "unclean" are probably intended.

. . . were all drawing near to hear him.

Jesus welcomed sinners! This was the issue for the Pharisees. He neither bought their favor nor joined with them in ethical compromises. Sinners knew where he stood but were nevertheless "drawn" to him.

And the Pharisees and the scribes murmured, saying,

Murmur is the same word used in the Greek Old Testament for the repeated "murmuring" of the people against Moses and Aaron in the wilderness (Exodus 15:24; 16:2, 7-8; 17:3; Numbers 14:2; 16:11). It appears only twice in the New Testament, here and in Luke 19:7. Both times it is in the mouth of Pharisees complaining against Jesus. The word has a special prefix *(dia)* that gives it an added edge. It is either "murmuring among themselves" or "murmuring through the crowd." We get the clear picture of an undercurrent of discontented complaining about Jesus' actions. These rumblings eventually crescendo in the events of the Passion.

"This man receives sinners and eats with them."

Receive in Greek also has a special prefix. The word *dechomai* means "to receive." But in this verse we have *prosdechomai,* which means "to welcome into fellowship." The first word would mean a willingness to sit down and talk with a person. The second means accepting him or her as a friend. It is

---

[4]For *sinners* see Mt 9:10-11; 11:19; Mk 2:15; Lk 5:30; 7:34. For *adulterers* see Mt 21:31-32; Lk 18:11. For *Gentiles* see Mt 18:17.

easy in any age to have long and continued dealings with a person and still never accept that person fully into fellowship. Paul uses this *prosdechomai* for welcoming a person as a sister or brother in the Lord (Romans 16:2; Philippians 2:29). The word appears in the sayings of Jesus, where Mark states, "Whoever receives one such child in my name receives me; and whoever receives me, receives not me but him who sent me" (Mark 9:37).

The crowning blow was that Jesus ate with them. In the eyes of his opponents Jesus was defiled by such contact. But there was more! To eat with another person in the Mideast is a sacramental act signifying acceptance on a very deep level. Many times over the decades I have stayed to partake of a meal in a village because of this reality. I neither wanted nor needed the food offered and could ill afford the time. By eating with a person, however, I was accepting that person on a basic and very fundamental level. If the guest is a religious teacher or leader, the villagers believe the guest imparts a semiphysical "blessing" by mere presence. All of this interchange was taking place between Jesus and classes of people carefully ostracized by the "righteous."

The big fight between Peter and Paul was over the question of eating. Paul tells his side of the story in Galatians 2:11-12. The issue was that Peter sat and ate with uncircumcised Gentile Christians and then withdrew from them! Friendship was one thing. To eat a meal with that friend was something else.

So he told them this parable. (Verse 3)

Luke introduces three stories with a singular. The three stories of Luke 15 are a single unit and were most likely composed as a unit by Jesus himself. In Luke 5:36-39 and Luke 6:39-41 similar units appear.

Them clearly refers to the scribes and Pharisees. Jesus was not talking to a general audience but rather to a very specific group of people who were upset because he welcomed outcasts into full fellowship with himself.

What man of you, having a hundred sheep, if he has lost one of them,
does not leave the ninety-nine in the wilderness, and go after
the one which is lost, until he finds it? (Verse 4)

This verse is a startling response to the complaint of the Pharisees. The Pharisees began as a lay movement, and they were expected to work for a living in some secular profession. One could not accept money for teaching the law. Thus Paul was a tentmaker and Jesus a carpenter, and thereby addressing Pharisees as "working men" was not a problem. But shepherds were considered unclean by the rabbis, who referred to such people as "people of the land" and avoided them.[5] Clearly Jesus did not consider shepherding an unclean profession.

A hundred sheep represented considerable wealth. The phrase "having a hundred sheep" can refer to ownership. It can also mean responsibility for a hundred sheep. In either case a scholar such as a Pharisee would hire a shepherd. Shepherds in the Middle East are poor men, clothed in simple dress, who wander in privation over the countryside. No educated man would spend his days tramping over the wilderness for any purpose. Pharisees no doubt expected Jesus to say something like this: "Which of you, owning a hundred sheep, if you received a report that one was lost, would not send a servant to the shepherd responsible and threaten him with dismissal if he didn't find the sheep?"

Then also the story Jesus tells is best understood as a reshaping of Psalm 23, with himself at its center. This possibility turns this first parable into an amazing introduction to this trilogy of three stories. Jesus claims to be the divine presence among the people searching for the lost and thus fulfilling the promises of Psalm 23, Jeremiah 23:1-8 and Ezekiel 34:1-31.[6]

Jesus continues by saying, "If *he* has lost one of them." Arabic translations in the past have turned this into a passive to read "If one of them is lost," because at both ends of the Mediterranean *the speaker never blames himself.* In Arabic and in Spanish a person doesn't say "I missed the train," but rather "The train left me." Neither does someone say "I dropped the dish," but rather "The dish fell from my hand." Not "I lost my pen," but rather "The pen went from me." It took more than a thousand years for Arabic translators to overcome this common style of speech and give the reader the non-idiomatic phrase "If he has lost one of them," awkward though it is. As we will note, the shepherd, when addressing his friends, fell into this traditional style of speaking when he states, "The sheep which was lost."

Jesus broke the common speech patterns of the day by placing respon-

---

[5]Shepherds appear on the lists of "proscribed trades." See Joachim Jeremias, *Jerusalem in the Time of Jesus* (Philadelphia: Fortress, 1969), pp. 302-12.

[6]See Kenneth E. Bailey, *Jacob and the Prodigal* (Downers Grove, Ill.: InterVarsity Press, 2003), pp. 65-85.

sibility on the shepherd, saying "If *he* has lost one of them." This departure from traditional idiom is important. Jesus is saying to his audience, "You lost your sheep. I went after it and brought it home. Now you have the gall to come to me complaining! Don't you realize that I am making up for your mistakes?"

The ninety-nine sheep were left in the wilderness, perhaps with an under-shepherd and quite likely in a cave.[7] Yet was it wise to leave the ninety-nine and wander away searching for the one? Christian missionaries have debated this point with communist dialecticians in China. Does the lost individual matter or are "the people" alone important? Indeed, it is the shepherd's willingness to go after the one that gives the ninety-nine their real security. If the one is sacrificed in the name of the larger good of the group, then each individual in the group is insecure, knowing that he or she too is of little value. If lost, he or she will be left to die. When the shepherd pays a high price to find the one, he thereby offers the profoundest security to the many.

We do not know how long he searched. But any Lebanese or Palestinian peasant can tell you that it may take a day or more of climbing over rugged wilderness to find a lost sheep.[8] When money—our money—is lost, we will pay a high price to recover it. Lost people are often judged to be of less value.

And when he has found it, he lays it on his shoulders, rejoicing.

After finding the lost sheep the shepherd's hardest job was still before him because he had yet to carry the heavy beast back to the flock. Frankly, I am proud to have carried myself over those isolated rugged hills. Unsuspecting tourists who wander bravely off across that marginal land, camera in hand, are often taken out on stretchers. The shepherd takes up his heavy burden "rejoicing" and accepts this backbreaking task happily. It would be natural for the shepherd to secretly hope to find the animal dead or devoured by a lion. Then, like Amos, he could gather a few scraps of hide and bone as proof that he neither stole nor sold the beast (Amos 3:12). When the lost is found, *the task of restoration has barely begun.* This theme disappears in the second story only to reappear with all of its glorious fullness in

---

[7]Eric F. F. Bishop, *Jesus of Palestine: The Local Background to the Gospel Documents* (London: Lutterworth, 1955), p. 166.

[8]I have discussed this matter with many of them. After two days the animal is presumed to be stolen or killed and eaten by wild animals.

the third story. It is a crucial theme within which lies the cross.

He laid it on his shoulders. The Middle Eastern shepherd has always carried a sheep over his two shoulders with its stomach against the back of his neck and all four feet tied together in front of his face. This gives him full control of the animal and still leaves one hand free for climbing. The early church often represented Jesus as the Good Shepherd. Such statues and paintings always depict the shepherd with a sheep around his neck. The Coptic section of the Greco-Roman museum in Alexandria, Egypt, has a moving, life-size marble statue of the Good Shepherd in just such a pose. The Rocke-feller Museum just north of Old Jerusalem has a similar statue, and in each case the sheep is large and the shepherd smiling. A fresco in a Christian church excavated at Dura-Europos, which was destroyed by the Persians A.D. 256, has the same scene, and the sheep is larger than the shepherd. In all of these early Eastern artistic presentations of the Good Shepherd, the price paid is emphasized by the extraordinary size of the sheep. Clearly Christ's passion is foreshadowed in this text and in these representations of it.

In the West the Good Shepherd is depicted in innumerable stained-glass windows. He usually has a young lamb in the crook of his arm. This may be adequate for the picture of Yahweh in Isaiah 40:11. It has little to do with the Good Shepherd of Luke 15, which tells of the price the shepherd pays to save his lost sheep.

> *And when he comes home, he calls together*
> *his friends and his neighbors, saying to them, "Rejoice with me,*
> *for I have found my sheep which was lost." (Verse 6)*

The shepherd returns to the village and rejoices *with the community*. This is understandable in light of the fact that, as noted below, the flock is quite possibly partly owned by those same "friends and neighbors." In village society the houses on a narrow village street are usually occupied by one family clan. Such a village clan may include ten to twenty families. Each household will own a few sheep, which produce the wool for their winter clothing. The entire alley together may have a hundred sheep, and naturally they are all concerned for the welfare of the flock. The loss of a sheep from the flock is a matter of concern for the entire community.[9] The extended family and com-

---

[9]Bishop, *Jesus of Palestine*, p. 166. My own experience confirms Bishop's views.

munity sustain the loss and then rejoice together when the lost is found. Even so, the lost person is a loss to the entire family of God. When an individual is lost, the community should mourn, and the "shepherd" who returns, restoring that person, should receive a joyous hero's welcome from his "friends."[10]

The Pharisees, as religious leaders, were indeed the "shepherds of Israel." Thus it is easy to see that in this parable Jesus is holding them responsible for any "sheep" (read: person) that is lost from the community. In the parable the shepherd does four things:

1. He accepts responsibility for the loss.

2. He searches without counting the cost.

3. He rejoices in the burden of restoration.

4. He rejoices with the community at the success of restoration.

Jesus here sets a high standard for the church in any age.

Just so, I tell you, there will be more joy in heaven over
one sinner who repents than over ninety-nine righteous persons
who need no repentance. (Verse 7)

Jesus' subtle humor is evident in this verse. The "righteous" who "need no repentance" do not exist. Naturally, heaven's joy over them will be minimal. As the parable concludes, the ninety-nine sheep are still in the wilderness! How can the village community rejoice over sheep that are not yet home? The Pharisees should have remembered Isaiah's words, "All we like sheep have gone astray" (Isaiah 53:6), and the words of the preacher in Ecclesiastes who wrote, "Surely there is not a righteous man on earth who does good and never sins" (Ecclesiastes 7:20).

But more important is the fact that the lost sheep is clearly symbolic of a repentant sinner. This comes as a complete surprise. How can this sheep represent "repentance"? Quite simple, Jesus is defining repentance as "acceptance of being found." The sheep is discovered to be missing. The shepherd pays the price to search for, find and restore the lost sheep. Terrified

---

[10]The word *friends* is a key word. The Pharisees formed into "clubs" in the villages. These clubs were called *Khaburim* (Friends). Jesus is saying "You are the 'Friends,' and you should rejoice with me when I find a lost sheep, just as the friends of the shepherd in my parable rejoice with him."

and alone, the sheep is overjoyed to be found and in the process becomes a symbol for repentance. Repentance is not a work which earns our rescue. Rather, the sinner accepts being found.

One form of oriental logic is to build up a series of similar illustrations to make a point (see Amos 3:3-8; 1 Corinthians 9:7-12). So here there are three parables on the same topic. Some dramatic elements remain constant through all three, others develop and still others shift in emphasis. For example, the first and the third stories stop but don't close. All three parables have the same three symbolic references. Clearly the lost sheep symbolizes sinners in their need, and the Good Shepherd is a symbol for Jesus. The ninety-nine represent the audience. But in this first story the ninety-nine are left "in the wilderness." How could the shepherd enjoy a party with his friends when the ninety-nine remained unaccounted for? He is expected to deposit the one lost sheep and return at once to the wilderness to bring home the rest of the flock. This huge hole in the first story is finally closed in the third story, as we will see. This brings us to the second parable.

> *"Or what woman, having ten silver coins, if she loses one coin,*
> *does not light a lamp and sweep the house and seek diligently*
> *until she finds it? And when she has found it,*
> *she calls together her friends and neighbors, saying,*
> *'Rejoice with me, for I have found the coin which I had lost.'*
> *Just so, I tell you, there is joy before the angels of God over*
> *one sinner who repents." (Verses 8-10)*

Jesus is still talking about money. Whenever money is involved, people's reactions are often visceral and uncomplicated by hypocrisy. But the most striking fact of this parable is its very existence. If Jesus is the Good Shepherd, then Jesus is also the Good Woman. Clearly this is what he intends his listeners to conclude. Jesus who had both men and women as disciples wanted his message to resonate deep within the hearts of all his listeners. Hence this pair of stories. So, what is the cultural setting of the parable of the lost coin?

Middle Eastern peasant women occasionally carry their worldly wealth in gold or silver coins fastened to a chain around their necks. This jewelry is referred to as "the women's bank." Literally millions of dollars are tied up in this kind of capital. If divorced or widowed, this wealth will help sustain her.

When her husband gives her a gift, it may be another pierced coin or medallion. Some commentators have suggested this custom as a background for the parable.

But there is a more probable alternative. Peasant women carry any cash held for daily expenses in a tightly knotted rag. The drachma mentioned in this story is a Greek coin weighing 4.3 grams of silver.[11] It was a day's wages for a laborer. Perhaps these ten coins were given to the wife to provide for the family for a week or two. She tied them up in her little rag but the knot worked loose and a coin fell out. Having failed to be more careful, she was filled with shame and remorse for not tying her rag more tightly. The village homes of the early centuries around the sea of Galilee often had floors made of either a lime plaster or of smooth uncut stones from the sea of Galilee. Cracks naturally developed in such floors and coins often fell into those cracks, becoming a delight for modern archeologists who find them. Windows in peasant homes of the period were small slits placed about seven feet up the wall from the floor. The building stone around the sea of Galilee is a very black basalt, which would have added to the darkness of the home. Even in broad daylight the woman naturally needed a lamp to find a coin.

Part of what drove her frantic search was the realization that she had lost the coin in the house. She knows this to be the case because that day she had not been out.

The lost sinners Jesus was receiving were in the house of Israel, not in a far country. They were a part of the "wealth" of the nation and could be found. If Jesus' critics would seek diligently they too could find the lost.

The woman is even more responsible for the loss of her coin than the shepherd was for the lost sheep. The shepherd could be excused. After all, he had one hundred sheep. The sheep, to a certain extent, have a will of their own and the wilderness was vast. But the peasant woman can blame no one but herself. All through her search she mutters repeatedly, *How stupid of me! Why didn't I secure the coin on its chain more firmly?* Or as I prefer, *Why didn't I tie my cloth more tightly?* Her remorse and desperation stem from this sense of undeniable responsibility, and her joy, like the shepherd's, cries out to be shared.

---

[11]By Luke's day this coin was out of circulation, having been replaced by the denarius. Luke records the archaic word used in the original telling. This is not Luke's story. He is merely faithfully reporting a story of Jesus.

The woman openly accepts responsibility for having lost her coin (unlike the shepherd). To his friends, the shepherd spoke of "my sheep which was lost." By contrast the woman openly tells her friends, "I have found the coin which I had lost."

The story provides a brief, intimate glance of village life. The genders of the words used tell us that the shepherd had a party only for men, and the woman had a celebration solely for women. Following the mores of the culture, it would be quite improper for either of them to mix socially with members of the opposite sex. Also village life is delightfully full of simple joys. A woman finding a lost coin is a big event that merits a party. She could relate how she lost the coin, when she discovered her loss, where she searched and how she felt when she finally saw it glinting there in the soft light of the oil lamp. The finding of a lost tax collector should have stimulated similar joyous excitement.

The listener or reader is now expected to ponder this pair of stories. As noted, all three major players are on stage, but they are mute. Neither sheep nor coins can talk. At this point we are in the midst of a double progression. In the first story the lost is *one in a hundred.* In the second story it is *one in ten,* and in the parable of the prodigal son it is *one in two.* The second progression is in regard to the availability of the place where the lost article can be found. The lost sheep is in the wide wilderness; the coin is confined to the house. But the sons are lost as they fall out of the circle of a father's love.

The actors and the people they represent is found in figure 1.

Actors in the Drama	The Lost Sheep	The Lost Coin	The Lost Son
Jesus	the shepherd	the woman	the father
irreligious sinners	lost sheep	lost coin	the prodigal
Pharisees	ninety-nine	the nine	the older son

Figure 1. Three parables of Luke 15

This brings us to the third story, which is the climax of the three.

CHAPTER TWO

The Death Wish

In this plate, reading from the bottom, the son requests his share of the family wealth while his father is still alive. To do so means he wants his father to die.

We expect him to ask for his "inheritance." Although he considered this option briefly, he crosses it out. He does not want the responsibility that such a request would entail. He substitutes a long, wordy circumlocution. His speech is like an ascending staircase that leads to an imagined freedom. The last step is the word *Wealth*.

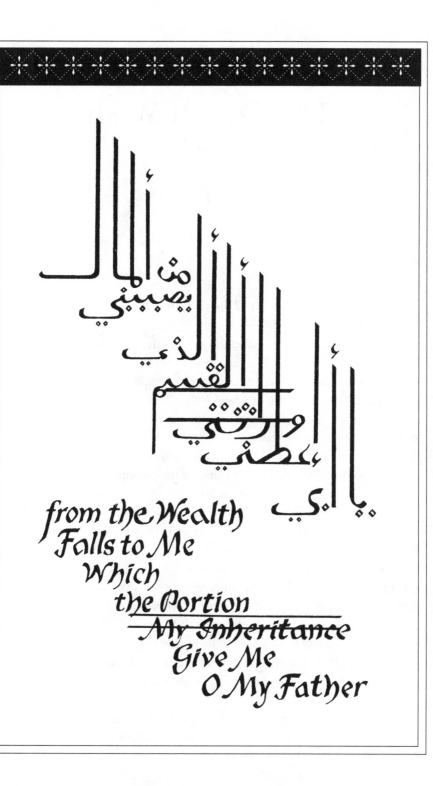

2

The Death Wish

LUKE 15:11-12

And he said, "There was a man who had two sons." (Verse 11)

This parable is traditionally called the story of the prodigal son. Some see it as two stories. The first tells of a son who runs away. Then at the end, a shorter, less important story is added about the older son who stays at home. Such is not the case. Our text opens with: "There was a man who had two sons." All three major players are mentioned in the opening phrase of the story. We cannot neglect any of them. The interrelationships between all three are supremely important. The older son is clearly as important as his younger brother. Perhaps a better name for the parable would be "The Compassionate Father and the Two Lost Sons."

The climax of the whole story occurs in the courtyard at the end, where the father stands pleading with his older son. Thus the older brother's relationships need careful scrutiny from the very beginning. His anger at both his father and his brother that appears at the end of the story is not a root out of dry ground. When seen through peasant eyes, certain key factors emerge. These will be examined as we proceed.

And the younger of them said to his father,
"Father, give me the share of property that falls to me."
And he divided his living between them. (Verse 12)

Such a request in village society means only one thing: *The younger son is impatient for his father's death.* The division of the father's wealth would naturally come only at the very end of the father's life as happened in the story of Abraham (Genesis 25:5-8). In like manner, only as he sensed his approaching death did Jacob reflect on giving his "blessing" to his sons (Genesis 48—49).[1]

As Joachim Jeremias has pointed out, there were legal procedures available if the father chose to divide the property, but naturally these procedures were expected to be used only as death approached.[2] In such a case an heir was given the legal right of *possession,* but not the right of *disposition.* The property was his, but his father still had control over it. This is clearly the situation with the older son at the end of the parable where the father says, "All that is mine is yours." But at the same time the father still has the authority to order the slaughter of the calf. In the beginning the younger son demands and is granted the right both of possession and of disposition. But this is not the real issue.

Granted, the legal procedures were in place if the father chose to use them. But it is and most certainly was unthinkable for any son to request his portion of the family wealth while his father was still alive. Every Middle Eastern peasant understands this instinctively. With endless village groups all across the Middle East I have tested this thesis. The answer has always been the same. Again and again I have engaged in some form of the following conversation:

"Has anyone ever made such a request in your village?"
"Never!"
"Could anyone ever make such a request?"
"Impossible!"
"If anyone ever did, what would happen?"
"His father would become very angry and refuse!"
"Why?"
"This request means *he wants his father to die!*"

The universality of this ingrained concept strongly suggests that the attitude is of great antiquity. All across the Middle East, from Algeria to Iran and from the Sudan to Syria, the answer is the same. The biblical witness is in harmony with such an assumption.[3]

---

[1]Clearly this blessing was deeply related to his inheritance.
[2]Joachim Jeremias, *The Parables of Jesus* (New York: Scribner's, 1963), p 128.
[3]Beyond the Middle East, this attitude must surely be nearly universal. Does any culture anywhere condone such a request?

With this central fact in mind, we must examine what this verse tells the reader about all three principal characters in the drama.

The Younger Son

1. The request itself is a form of mutiny. The prodigal is impatient for his father to die. Theologically, Jesus is affirming that humankind in their rebellion against God really want him dead!

2. The prodigal is driven by a self-centered pride. He cries, "Give me the share of property that falls to me," implying "The devil take the rest of you." A traditional Middle Eastern village idiom affirms that a virtuous man "gives the right and takes the right." That is, an honorable man gives every other person a fair deal and expects the same from all. Later on the father will have a chance to start "taking his rights." But he chooses not to do so. Rather he offers an unexpected outpouring of love. At this point the prodigal thinks only of himself.

3. A relationship is broken, not a law. Deuteronomy 21:17 states that the younger son's portion is one third. The law does not specifically say that the son must wait for his father's death. The son has not broken the law. Rather he has broken his father's heart.

4. The prodigal doesn't seem to care how much others in the family will suffer because of what he demands. Not only will he hurt his father but also the entire family clan. The wealth of a village family is not held in stocks, bonds or savings accounts. Rather it is in a cluster of homes, in animals and in land. To suddenly lose one third of their total wealth would mean a staggering loss to the entire family clan. The parable specifically states that the prodigal settled his affairs in a few days. This means that he liquidated his assets in a hurry, which in turn indicates a "sale at any price." The accumulated economic gains of generations would be lost in a few days. In the East, where days are sometimes spent in bargaining over the smallest transaction, the man who sells in a hurry sells cheaply. The younger son is indifferent to all of these ramifications.

5. The younger son is also ungrateful. Although his father's love had been poured out on him, the agony of rejected love was his father's only reward.

6. There is no trust. The son takes his destiny into his own hands. He seems to feel that his father can no longer be trusted to direct his life.

7. The prodigal demands privilege without responsibility. He uses a long, wordy phrase. The direct natural request would have been "I want my in-

heritance." In Semitic languages this is said in two words. Rather he says, "Give me the share of property that falls to me" (in Arabic and Hebrew, six words). Why the long circumlocution? The word *inheritance* is seemingly carefully avoided. *Inheritance (klēronomia)* is used fourteen times in the New Testament, four times by Luke.[4] But here we have a rare word *(ousia)* that is used in this story and nowhere else in all of the New Testament. Again traditional Middle Eastern culture gives us the reason. To accept one's "inheritance" involves acceptance of leadership responsibility in the family clan. The recipient is duty bound to administer property and help solve family quarrels. He must defend the honor of the family against all comers (even with his life if necessary). He pledges himself to increase the clan's wealth and represent them nobly at village functions (such as weddings, feasts and funerals). He must "build the house of his father." But this is specifically what the younger son does not want and does not ask for. He wants the money! The word *ousia* can mean "wealth" and "property." It appears again in verse 13. Older translations used the general word *substance*. His share was most likely in property, which he turned to cash. He did not want or ask for his inheritance with the responsibility involved.

8. He cuts himself off from his roots as he seizes his share of the wealth and in the process breaks fellowship with his father. Thereby he cuts himself off from his real inheritance. The very inheritance he refused to ask for he has now forfeited. A man's security in the village is his family. This is as precious to him as life itself. His family is his social security, his insurance, his old-age pension, his assurance of marriage, his physical and emotional well-being; in short, it is everything. The tie to the land and to the "house of so-and-so" is a profound tie.

"Where are you from?" asks one city dweller of another. The answer is not his address. Rather he replies, "I am from such-and-such a village." He may never have been there, but his roots are there. His family clan is there. The "house" of which he is a part is established there. He belongs there. There he will be accepted totally, regardless. If he is out of work or in need of friends, he will be welcomed, even if they have never seen him. When he says, "I am so-and-so, son of so-and-so, and I am of the house of so-and-so," they will open their doors to him. All of this the younger son throws away. A man with no such roots is considered a vagabond and is not trusted.

---

[4]Mt 21:38; Mk 12:7; Lk 12:13; 20:14; Acts 7:5; 20:32; Gal 3:18; Eph 1:18; 5:5; Col 3:24; Heb 9:15; 11:8; 1 Pet 1:4.

To suggest that a man is "without roots" is an unpardonable insult. To borrow a distinction from medieval theology, the younger son has repudiated his substantial inheritance, and thus his accidental inheritance will eventually play out on him. He has substituted the passing for the permanent.

The richness of Jesus' imagery is significant. Indeed, God, our divine Father, offers the deepest kind of security to his children within the family clan. The "household of God" should mean to the believer what the extended family means to the Middle Eastern villager.

9. The younger son refuses to own his share in partnership with his father. When the boy is at home, all his father possesses is his also. But this is not sufficient for the rebel, who wants sole control over the money. He demands his share in complete separation from this partnership. The biblical understanding of possessions is permeated with this idea of ownership in partnership with the Father. The phrase in the Lord's Prayer "Give us this day our daily bread" presupposes such a worldview.

10. The younger son is himself totally responsible. We will have some hard things to say about his brother. Yet from the prodigal's point of view *he* is responsible. The sheep may have wandered away inadvertently. The coin was inanimate. But the son chose deliberately to wound his father's heart and break all his relationships with the family.

The Older Son

From the opening of the story we must also try to assess the feelings and attitudes of the older son. A number of things are evident:

1. He certainly knows the entire story. In a village community everything is known immediately by everyone. The conversation between the father and the younger son would have been overheard by the servants or other members of the family. Perhaps the older son himself was present. Many times, while talking in a village home to the members present in a room, I have been startled by an answering voice coming from another room or even from across the narrow street. The entire listening community around the speaker is part of the conversation even though not present in the room where the conversation is taking place. It is inconceivable that such a jarring incident would not be reported in the greatest detail to the older son. Indeed, every person in the entire village would hear it before sundown. When the prodigal starts to sell, all doubt is removed. The boy has been given his share.

Ecclesiastes reflects this kind of a world where it reads

Even in your thought, do not curse the king,
   nor in your bedchamber curse the rich;
for a bird of the air will carry your voice,
   or some winged creature tell the matter. (Ecclesiastes 10:20)

In short, everybody in the village knows everything.

2. The older son refuses to be the mediator. In a village quarrel the two parties never make up directly. To do so, someone would have to lose face, which is unthinkable. The process of reconciliation takes place through a third party, called "the mediator." This go-between fluctuates between one party and the other until he works out a solution that both sides can accept. There can be no winners or losers. The mediator then arranges a public meeting in which the two antagonists shake hands, embrace and kiss each other in token of reconciliation. The mediator is always selected on the basis of the strength of his relationships with the quarreling parties. In this case the older son would be the unspoken choice as a go-between.

In the villages when I come to this point in a sermon on this text, I always ask, "Who must be the reconciler?" The villagers always answer from their pews, "His brother, of course." Everybody knows this. Furthermore, he must start immediately. It is up to him to step in at once and try to reconcile his brother to his father. The family and community demand it. But our man is silent. He refuses to fulfill the sacred responsibility that village custom places on his shoulders. Clearly, for some reason he does not want reconciliation to take place. If he hated his brother, he would still fulfill this task for the sake of his father.

In the East personal relationships are supreme. For the sake of you, my friend, my relative, I am willing to do everything. The climax comes in relationship to one's father. For *his sake* I am duty bound to do everything and anything. But here the older son refuses. The refusal is a clear indication of his broken relationship with his father. Things are not as they should be between him and his brother or him and his father.

3. We can perhaps proceed cautiously to build on his silent refusal of duty. He may well be part of the reason why his brother is leaving. In the East, age is honored. One village proverb says, "He who has not an old man will buy an old man." It means if you don't have an old man in your family to direct your life, you had better buy one. Another proverb says, "He who

is a day older than you is a year wiser." The second person in authority over
you after your father is not your mother but rather your older brother. The
father is called "father of so-and-so," using the name of the oldest son. In
the Old Testament, when the father dies, the older brother is to receive the
lion's share of the inheritance and he assumes responsibility for the family.[5]
These privileges sometimes produce an insufferable arrogance. This may
be the background of this parable. The arrogance of the older brother may
well have contributed to the rupturing of the younger man's relationship
with his father.

4. When the younger son leaves the house, the older son is again silent.
We cannot build too much on this, because the brevity of the story. However, the father, because of his position of estrangement with his younger
son, cannot bid him goodbye. Custom would not allow it. The elder son
again is responsible. He would be expected to plead with him not to leave
and remind him of the father's love. He would say to him, for example, "My
brother, your father is an old man. You may not see him again. Do not leave
us. Your mother will go blind weeping. We cannot bear even the thought of
your departure." Then, if the boy is determined to leave, he must tell him
that their prayers are with him, invoke God's protection for the journey and
plead with him to return speedily.

The terrors of travel in the ancient Middle East were considerable. These
terrors remained even until the late nineteenth century, where a son who
traveled to a far country was considered traveling perhaps never to return.
When he did return, a great feast was held, and guns were fired in salute.
Even today I have seen touching scenes of farewell at the railroad station. It
looks as if the family is sending off their only son to die in the war. On in-
vestigating I find that the traveler is going to the nearby town thirty miles
away and will be back in a month. The terrors of travel and the heartache
of separation are made much keener by the close-knit fellowship of the village family. All of this ritual and background is missing. The father cannot
say these things because of his estrangement. The elder son refuses to say
them because of his attitude.

---

[5]Luke 12:13-21 records the parable of the rich fool. In the introduction a younger brother
presses Jesus to order his older brother to give him his share of the inheritance. Clearly the
father has died and the older brother has taken over the estate. The younger brother wants to
claim his share, but the older brother's power over him makes that impossible, thus his request
to Jesus.

The Father

What then can be said of the father, who by granting the request did what no village father is ever going to do. The expected reaction is refusal and punishment. Knowing what the request means, the father grants freedom even to turn away from him. William Temple has somewhere said that *God grants us freedom, even to reject his love.* But in addition, the father remains the father. He does not sever his relationship with his son. The relationship is broken because of the son's act, but the father still holds out his broken end of the rope of relationship hoping that the other end can yet be joined. In so doing he suffers. If the father had disowned the son, there would then be no possibility of reconciliation. The father's suffering provides the foundation of the possibility of the son's return. All of this makes abundantly clear that Jesus has not taken an oriental patriarch as a model for God. Rather he breaks all the bounds of patriarchal culture to present this matchless picture of a father who alone should shape our image of God as our heavenly father.

All three actors in our drama reveal their own character from the very start. We know the younger son by what he asks, the father by what he does, and the older son by what he does not do.

The text says: "He divided his living between *them*." The older son also receives his share at this time. The father is clearly still in authority. He grants the right of possession, but the older son does not press for the right of disposition. Yet from the start each son is assigned his share of the family property. This is crucial for understanding the older brother's reaction at the end of the story.

CHAPTER THREE

The Face-Saving Plan

The prodigal is desperate. He has to eat somehow. Finally he decides on a face-saving plan. He will go home and work as a craftsman. Living independently, he will be able to avoid his brother.

After acquiring a skill, he will be able to earn money, pay his father back and thus save himself through his own effort. He has no genuine humility; he just wants to eat. From right to left the faces begin with a show of remorse and end with a wry smile.

3

The Face-Saving Plan

LUKE 15:13-19

Not many days later, the younger son gathered all he had
and took his journey into a far country, and there
he squandered his property in loose living. (Verse 13)

The prodigal must "get out of town" in a hurry. The reason is clear. He moves around the village trying to "sell his birthright for a mess of pottage" as he exchanges his inheritance for a sack of gold coins. The words *gathered all (synagagōn panta)* literally mean "turned everything into cash."[1] The New English Bible translates this verse: "A few days later the younger son turned the whole of his share into cash and left home for a distant country." The scorn of the entire community would have been considerable, hence the rush to sell and get out of town. He leaves, and the only thing that follows him is the love of his brokenhearted father.

But there is more.

First century Jewish custom dictated that if a Jewish boy lost the family inheritance among the Gentiles and dared to return home, the community would break a large pot in front of him and cry out "so-in-so is cut off from his people." This ceremony was called the *Kezazah* (literally "the cutting off"). After it was performed, the community would have nothing to do with

---

[1]William F. Arndt and F. Wilbur Gingrich, "συνάγω," in *A Greek-English Lexicon of the New Testament and Other Early Christian Literature* (Chicago: University of Chicago, 1957), p. 789.

the wayward person.[2] By selling his inheritance and taking it with him the prodigal takes a huge risk; if he loses that money among the Gentiles, he burns his bridges and has no way to return home. He has no more "rights" to claim and no one will take him in.

He travels to a far country. The Greek word for "took his journey" *(apedēmēsen)* is a colorful term that literally means: "He traveled away from his own people." Luke uses the word only here. The younger son has indeed left his own people. It is pointless to speculate as to where the "far country" might have been, but we do know that it is among the Gentiles because they ate pork and used pigs as sacrificial animals. The listener or reader remembers that the *Kezazah* ceremony awaits him if he loses the money in such a community.

In the far country he "squandered his property." The word "squandered" *(dieskorpisen)* means "scattered." It is used for the scattering of an enemy on the field of battle. It also refers to the scattering of a flock of sheep, the scattering of grain in the winnowing process, the scattering of seed in sowing and the wasting of money.[3] There is no record of how he "scattered" his money. The long interpretive tradition that assumed the prodigal spent his resources in immoral ways is built on his older brother's slanderous remarks. But actually, the older brother knows nothing, and the parable is silent on the matter. All the reader knows is that the money was wasted. Furthermore the phrase *zōn asōtōs,* translated "loose living," has as its basic meaning "spendthrift living." Aristotle describes a prodigal thus: "A 'prodigal' means a man who has a single evil quality, that of wasting his substance."[4]

From the everyday use of this word in the early centuries, we have a record of a public notice in which a man's parents announced that their son "by riotous living" had squandered all his own property.[5] In another case a wife lays a complaint against her husband for misuse of her property.[6] Werner Foerster writes: "In terms of the general Gk. usage, *zōn asōtōs* at Lk. 15:7 speaks of the dissipated life of the Prodigal without specifying the na-

---

[2]Kenneth E. Bailey, *Jacob and the Prodigal* (Downers Grove, Ill.: InterVarsity Press, 2003), p. 102 n. 8.

[3]See Mt 25:24; 26:31; Mk 14:27; Lk 1:51; 16:1; Acts 5:37.

[4]Aristotle *Nicomachean Ethics* 4.1.1119[b], *The Works of Aristotle* 2, Great Books of the Western World, ed. Robert Maynard Hutchins (Chicago: Encyclopaedia Britannica, 1952), 9:366.

[5]James Hope Moulton and George Milligan, *The Vocabulary of the Greek Testament Illustrated from the Papyri and Other Non-literary Sources* (Grand Rapids: Eerdmans, 1952), p. 89.

[6]Ibid.

ture of this life, cf. v. 30. It is simply depicted as carefree and spendthrift in contrast to the approaching dearth."[7]

This is the only place in the New Testament where this adverb is used. For centuries the Arabic translations have read, "extravagant living."

If the prodigal is a traditional Middle Eastern villager, his pattern of behavior can be understood and reconstructed. The money is used primarily to establish a reputation for generosity. He holds large banquets and gives out expensive gifts. Generosity is a supreme virtue, coveted by all. The opportunity to gain status in the eyes of new friends through an exercise of this virtue would be the highest kind of pleasure for such an individual. But he eats the fruit of a tree he has left unwatered to die. He has transplanted his palm tree into cement.

And when he had spent everything, a great famine arose in that country, and he began to be in want. (Verse 14)

Luke selects his vocabulary very carefully. The word *spent* is again a special word that means "waste" or "squander" or "spend freely." The imagery of verse 13 is continued. When the younger son's "accidental" inheritance runs out and the specter of famine hovers over him like a threatening storm cloud, he realizes that he is in big trouble. So why not go home? This would be the most natural solution to his problems. But our younger son will not do so, not yet. Why? There are at least two reasons that keep him in the far country.

First, at home he would have to endure his brother's scorn. Not only will he be blamed for the past but also, if he returns, he will be obliged to live off his brother's inheritance. He will "eat his brother's bread" and thereby be indebted to his father *and* to his brother, whose hostility will increase. This cup is too bitter; he cannot drink it, at least not yet. His estrangement from his brother keeps him from fellowship with his father.

Second, he must face the village. He has broken his relationships with the entire community and is now despised by all. Life in their midst is painful to contemplate. Having broken the rules and "lost his inheritance among the Gentiles," the *Kezazah* ceremony now threatens. Village society is ruthless with the man who is down. Wandering beggars endure unspeakable taunt-

---

[7]Werner Foerster, "ἀσώτως, ἀσωτία," in *Theological Dictionary of the New Testament*, ed. Gerhard Kittel, trans. Geoffrey W. Bromiley (Grand Rapids: Eerdmans, 1964), 1:507.

ing. Village children play in the streets and are always ready to follow any unfortunate through the village, clapping in mockery and shouting a taunt song as they go.

Mark 10:46-52 records the story of Jesus' mercy on Bartimaeus. The name Timaeus quite likely comes from the Hebrew root meaning "unclean." So Bartimaeus would mean "Son of Filth." This was the taunt name the local populace gave this beggar.

Another instance of village mockery is found in the story of Elisha and a gang of boys. The prophet Elisha was apparently bald. Even though he was a prophet, he was not spared the mockery of the village children. The text reads:

> He went up from there to Bethel; and while he was going up on the way, some small boys came out of the city and jeered at him, saying, "Go up, you baldhead! Go up, you baldhead!" And he turned around, and when he saw them, he cursed them in the name of the LORD. And two she-bears came out of the woods and tore forty-two of the boys. (2 Kings 2:23-24)

The prophet was exceedingly severe in his retaliation, but when someone has seen and experienced the verbal cruelty of a village gang, with its scoffing and derisive choruses, that person almost delights in reading that once, long ago, they were dealt with. In Palestinian villages I have had men from the village, thinking I was an Arab pilgrim and thereby a guest in their town, escort me through their village to keep the "gang" at a distance. The prodigal will have to face this band. He will be verbally attacked by it, only in his case the adults will join the mockery rather than protect him from it. He had lost his inheritance among the Gentiles!

The parable says "a great famine arose in that country." Our twenty-first century world knows famines. But at least there are communications and an international community available to assist with aid. But before such capabilities were available, a great famine in the Middle East was an indescribable horror. One such famine occurred in 1889 in Sudan. At that time Sudan was cut off from the outside world by the successful revolution of a religious leader called the *Mahdi*. An Austrian officer named Rudolf Carl von Slatin was trapped in Sudan by the revolt. In the summer of 1889 famine struck. Von Slatin later escaped and recorded his experiences.[8] He tells of children

---

[8]Rudolf Carl von Slatin, *Fire and Sword in the Sudan, 1879-1895* (London: Edward Arnold, 1907), pp. 453-56.

being sold into slavery to keep them from starving. He speaks of people found dead every morning on the streets of Omdurman, the capital city. When the numbers increased, the ruler of the city declared every man responsible for throwing the dead in front of his house into the river. The inhabitants of the Omdurman then tried to drag the corpses from in front of their houses over to the neighbors. Each morning quarrels rang out across the city as men fought over where the dead really died. Merchants had to keep hippopotamus-hide whips nearby to drive off the maddened beggars who would attack them bodily and ravish their shops. Small merchants with their wares on the streets would throw themselves across their wares as these miserable wretches came by. Unarmed men venturing out at night were attacked and eaten. Straying animals were killed and eaten raw. Shoe leather, rotten flesh and garbage were all devoured; even palm trees were consumed. Village families, seeing death upon them, bricked up the doors of their houses and awaited death in an inner room to keep their bodies from being devoured by hyenas. Entire villages were wiped out in this manner. Such recollections would have been in the memories of Jesus' audience. The prodigal will endure almost anything rather than forfeit his pride and return in humiliation to his family and the home village.

So he went and joined himself to one of the citizens of that country,
who sent him into his fields to feed swine. (Verse 15)

The verb translated "joined" is used in the New Testament in this simple sense of one man joining another. However, the word itself *(kollaō)* comes from the word glue *(kolla)* and can also be translated: "he clung to" or "he attached himself to." Indeed, the prodigal glued himself to a citizen of that country. The word is used of a man "joining" himself to his wife, of dust that "clings" to the feet, of "joining" to a prostitute, and of "holding fast" to what is good. The verb is used twelve times in the New Testament, and seven of these appear in Luke's writings.[9]

This typically oriental practice persists to this day. In a crowded city center you park your car. A man appears from the teeming swarms in the street. He opens your door and begins furiously to polish your already-clean windshield. He grabs any bag out of your hand and follows you into a store. All

---

[9]See Lk 10:11; 15:15; Acts 5:13; 8:29; 9:26; 10:28; 17:34.

efforts to shake him are futile. He picks up your purchases from the counter and returns with you to the car. He expects, of course, to be paid hand-somely for his "loyal and faithful services." He has "glued" himself to you. So it is in our story.

The citizen in the far country most likely doesn't want the prodigal at all and tries to get rid of him by offering him a job he is confident the beggar will refuse. This is standard Middle Eastern practice. A school principal who wants to dismiss a teacher does not fire the teacher. Instead the principal assigns the teacher a task which he knows the teacher will refuse. A com-pany wishing to fire an employee offers a transfer to some faraway village. They know the employee will refuse and resign. Even so, the citizen of the far country probably wants nothing to do with this beggar in that there are many such beggars coming to his door each day. This particular young man is known in the community. He must be from an upper-class family because he arrived with wealth. They know from his dress and speech that he is a Jew. This means that he abhors swine. If he has any honor left, he will refuse to feed them. The Middle East still detests the pig: the Muslim and the Jew by the dictates of religion, the Christian, for the most part, by choice. The repulsiveness of the notion of feeding swine, for someone whose culture and tradition loathes pigs is difficult to communicate. In discussing farming with villagers I have often been reticent and sometimes embarrassed to ad-mit that my countrymen raise pigs. But the prodigal is desperate. He accepts.

The text tells us that the owner of the pigs is a "citizen." This means he is a man of some means and position. Not all inhabitants of a country were citizens. The word used here most likely refers to that special class of the privileged few who had full rights in the city government of one of the Greek cities of the Middle East. Luke, well-educated in Greek, is the only Gospel writer to use this word (see Luke 15:15; 19:14; Acts 21:39).

Some Christian villages in the Middle East keep pigs as community "gar-bage collectors." They run loose in the streets and feed on garbage and ma-nure. The modern farmer, with his nicely fenced pig lots and concrete feed-ing slabs, is a million miles away in thought and in practice from the world of our parable.

> *And he would gladly have fed on the pods that the swine ate;*
> *and no one gave him anything. (Verse 16)*

The prodigal desperately wanted to eat the pods that he was throwing to the pigs, but his stomach could not digest them. The Greek word behind "would gladly" is a strong word. Its meanings include "desire," "lust," "craving" and "longing." It also refers to sexual desire. This word appears when Jesus says, "With *desire* I have *desired* to eat this Passover" (Luke 22:15).

Furthermore, as a Jew the prodigal probably could not bring himself to eat the scraps of pig meat that were left for the shepherds when an animal from the herd was butchered by the citizen master. To feed pigs was revolting enough! To eat their entrails was unthinkable!

The verse does not say that the son *ate* the pods but merely indicates that he earnestly *desired* to do so. He longed to be a pig so that he could digest the coarse pods the pigs were eating.[10] The pigs were better off than he. Their bellies were full while his was empty.

Clearly he tried begging. Carts and people use the roads as well as herds. He probably followed each passing party as far as he dared and, with hand outstretched, emitted a pitiful, pleading whine to no avail in that "no one gave him anything."

His despair reached a new depth. He was not at the end of his rope—not yet. But his utter want finally overcame the shame he would feel before his father, his brother and the village. The brutal gauntlet through which he must pass in the village was now unavoidable. He was starving, and a man has to eat somehow!

He did not seriously consider returning home, in any capacity, until after all other alternatives were tried and found hopeless. As he would soon be too weak to walk home, he must return while he still had strength enough to make the journey.

But when he came to himself, he said, "How many of my father's hired
servants have bread enough and to spare, but I perish here with hunger!
I will arise and go to my father, and I will say to him,
'Father, I have sinned against heaven and before you;
I am no longer worthy to be called your son;
treat me as one of your skilled craftsman.' " (Verses 17-19)

---

[10]The word for "pods" is *keratiōn,* which may refer to the seed pods of the carob tree (Ceratonia siliqua), a variety of locust or acacia. These pods can be boiled to make a karob treacle. A human cannot survive on the pods themselves. Pigs can.

The younger son finally "came to himself" and decided to return home. For centuries this phrase has been interpreted to mean "he repented." But did he? In his soliloquy in the far country he expressed no remorse, *only* a desire to eat. He did not say "I shamed my family" or "I caused my father deep pain and anguish." He doesn't even voice regret that he lost the money. While talking to himself he thinks, in effect, *Others eat while I am hungry. I must do something.* Some Arabic versions have translated it as "he got smart." For 1,800 years Arabic and Syriac versions have never used language in this text that implies repentance.

His problem is that he had lost the money among the Gentiles and knew that he would be confronted with the *Kezazah* ceremony on his return home. Restoration to the family and community was only possible, (he assumed) after he paid back the money he had lost. But he had no marketable skills. Hence his plan to seek job training so that he could join the work force. Only then could he save his money (like other craftsmen), compensate for his losses and one day again take his place in the family and community.

But to be accepted as an apprentice with a craftsman he would need his father's backing. The game plan therefore was to make a "very humble speech" that would (he hoped) convince his father to back him—just once more!

Sadly, the prodigal does not yet understand the nature of his sin. He thinks the issue is the lost money. It isn't! It is the father's broken heart. The problem is not the broken law but the broken relationship. If he is a servant, he can get a job, earn the money and pay his debts. But if he is a son of the house, such a solution will not satisfy his father. As yet he understands none of this. Hence the nature of his proposed "confession."

The planned opening remark in his speech was carefully selected. He prepared to say, "Father, I have sinned before heaven and your sight." Jesus was addressing a scholarly audience. This sentence is a paraphrase from the mouth of Pharaoh when he addressed Moses after the first nine plagues. As pressure mounted on Pharaoh to deal with Moses, he finally relented and summoned the prophet and confessed, "I have sinned against the LORD your God, and against you" (Exodus 10:16). The language of the Aramaic version of this text is even closer to Luke 15:18 than the Hebrew.[11] Everyone knows

---

[11]The *Targum Onkelos* introduces the word *qadam* ("in the presence of") which appears in Lk 15:18 in the Greek word *enōpion* which has the same meaning. Neither the word *qadam* nor its equivalent appear in the Hebrew text. See Alexander Sperber, *The Bible in Aramaic* (Leiden: Grill, 1959), 1:105.

that Pharaoh was not sincerely repenting. Rather he was trying to manipulate Moses into serving Pharaoh's interests. The appearance of a new version of this well known statement from the mouth of Pharaoh makes clear that the prodigal had a similar intent. He wanted to manipulate his father into trusting him—just once more—and endorsing him for job training with a reputable craftsman so that he could earn his way. He wanted no grace—he can manage on his own! He did not offer to become a slave *(doulos)*. Slaves are not paid. He needed money and asked to be trained as a *misthios* (a skilled craftsman).[12]

He remembered that the hired servants had "bread enough and to spare." Bread is the staple food in the village. Every meal consists of bread eaten with some other food.

Middle Eastern villagers eat their meals by breaking off small pieces of bread, one at a time, and dipping them into the common dish and eating them. The very word *bread* has strong emotional overtones missing in English. The villager says, "We are a people who eat bread." He means, "We are poor and have very little else to eat." A man does not work to "make a living." Rather he works to "eat bread." Middle Eastern speech is full of idiomatic references to bread. Life itself is called "the eating of bread." These attitudes toward bread are embedded throughout the Old and New Testaments. In the book of Job the wicked person is described as one who "wanders abroad for bread, saying, 'Where is it?'" (Job 15:23), and Judas is referred to by Jesus as "He who ate my bread has lifted his heel against me" (John 13:18). In the Lord's Prayer we ask for bread, not food.

"Bread enough and to spare" is more than many dare hope for. The prodigal remembers that in his father's house even the employed craftsmen enjoy this rare luxury.

There is a finely tuned nuance added to the story by the use of the word *arise.* As a prelude to his self-serving plan the prodigal thinks to himself, *I will arise and go.* A "resurrection" is needed, and at this point he thinks that he can accomplish that resurrection on his own. This same word will reappear in the mouth of his father with stunning power.

In the far country, as the prodigal uses this freighted word there is no contemplation of reconciliation or restoration to sonship. Before the story ends there will be a genuine "resurrection," at the edge of the village accomplished by his father's costly love.

---

[12]Kenneth E. Bailey, *Poet and Peasant and Through Peasant Eyes* (Grand Rapids: Eerdmans, 1980), p. 176-77.

A number of subtle attitudes appear on the negative side of the prodigal's confession. A brief summary of them may be helpful. His intended request for job training as a craftsman means many things. Among them are the following:

1. He will not live in the family home but rather in a nearby village with other blue-collar craftsmen. Thus life with his hated brother will not be necessary. If his plan is accepted, that same hatred will keep him from the fellowship of his father. He cannot live with his father without accepting his father's other son as a brother. If the unlovely brother would just leave the house, his problem would be much simpler.

2. As a paid craftsman he hopes to "make up" for what he has lost. In biblical times it was common practice for a man in debt to sell himself for a specified period of time in payment of his debts (see Leviticus 25:39-55; 2 Kings 4:1; Matthew 18:25). The prodigal lost the family money but hopes to redeem himself without help. Once the debt is paid he will regain the respect of the village. His father will surely be impressed with his "humility" at the beginning of the process and with his self-generated success at its end.

3. He anticipates a servant-master relationship with his father. With his mindset this is probably all he understands. At the beginning of the story the prodigal refused the responsibilities of his inheritance. That initial refusal makes clear that he also rejected authentic sonship. Sonship versus servanthood was a basic issue between Jesus and his Pharisee audience. It is a basic issue today between Christianity and Islam. Are we God's servants and he a law-giving Master? Or are we his beloved children and he a compassionate Father?

4. The prodigal does not yet see that the real issue is not a broken law (the money) but a broken *relationship*. He does not yet understand what he has done and what it really means. In the far country the job-training proposal seems like an excellent plan. He has not faced the fact that he broke his father's heart. Thus the problem of the healing of that broken heart does not occur to him. If he can return the money, he imagines that all will be well.

5. Reconciliation is not a part of his immediate plan. He wants to eat and says so. He is working as a servant in the far country and is starving. He might as well get some job training, establish himself in a new trade, earn a decent salary and be able to eat. Because he has not yet faced his own sin,

he cannot possibly understand what reconciliation means or what it costs.

In the deepest sense the prodigal is not going home. He is going back to servanthood. As long as his former attitudes remain, he is still in a far country spiritually even as he physically approaches his home village. In short, at the edge of the village he is still lost.

CHAPTER FOUR

The Shattering Confrontation

Whenever "O my Father" is brought together with "I have sinned," there is a cross.

Like the second plate, this speech also begins "O my Father." Only now the prodigal's words move down across the page. As rehearsed in the far country, they were an attempt to manipulate. Here, at the edge of the village, the speech is revised through omission, and the attempt to manipulate emerges as a sincere confession of unworthiness.

The father's cross of suffering was always there. Only now, after the shattering confrontation on the road, does the prodigal see it.

يا أبي أخطأت ولست مستحقًا

O my Father I have Sinned
And I am Unworthy

4

The Shattering
Confrontation

LUKE 15:20-24

And he arose and came to his father.
But while he was yet at a distance, his father saw him and had compassion,
and ran and embraced him and kissed him. (Verse 20)

Things didn't work out the way the son anticipated. What did happen was radically unorthodox from every perspective. The boy disgraced himself at the beginning of the story by requesting his inheritance and debased himself even further by selling it.

As the prodigal returned to the village he expected his father to remain aloof in the house while he made his way through the village. To say the least, he would be "subdued" in the process by the crowd in the street.

As soon as they discovered that the money had been lost among the Gentiles the *Kezazah* ceremony would be enacted. The son would then be obliged to sit for some time outside the gate of the family home before being allowed to even see his father. Finally he would be summoned. With the boy already rejected by the village, the father would be very angry, and the boy would be obliged to apologize for everything as he pleaded for job training in the next village.

But this is not what happens. No one in the village thinks or acts as a separate person but as a part of the tightly knit village society. The individual's solidarity with that community is unshakable. The father, however, reacts in a very countercultural manner. He breaks all the rules of oriental patriarchy as he runs down the road to reconcile his son to himself.

The word *run* in Greek *(dramōn)* is the technical term used for the foot-races in the stadium. Paul uses this word a number of times in this sense (1 Corinthians 9:24, 26; Galatians 2:2; 5:7; 2 Thessalonians 3:1; Hebrews 12:1). Luke is a well-educated man who chooses his words carefully. Thus we can translate the phrase, "His father saw him and had compassion and *raced.*" It is not just a slow shuffle or a fast walk—he races! In the Middle East a man of his age and position *always* walks in a slow, dignified fashion. It is safe to assume that he has not run anywhere for any purpose for forty years. No villager over the age of twenty-five ever runs. But now the father *races* down the road. To do so, he must take the front edge of his robes in his hand like a teenager. When he does this, his legs show in what is considered a humiliating posture. All of this is painfully shameful for him. The loiterers in the street will be distracted from tormenting the prodigal and will instead run after the father, amazed at seeing this respected village elder shaming himself publicly. It is his "compassion" that leads the father to race out to his son. He knows what his son will face in the village. He takes upon himself the shame and humiliation due the prodigal.

It is not possible to capture in any parable the mystery and wonder of God in Christ. Yet in this matchless story we have a clear indication of at least a part of what these things mean. The father, in his house, clearly represents God. The best understanding of the text is to see that when the father leaves the house and takes upon himself a humiliating posture on the road, he becomes a symbol of God incarnate. He does not wait for the prodigal to come to him but rather at great cost goes down and out to find and resurrect the one who is lost and dead. These actions (seen in a Middle Eastern context) clearly affirm one of the deepest levels of the meaning of both the incarnation and the atonement. Paul affirms the same truth with the great phrase, "in Christ God was reconciling the world to himself" (2 Corinthians 5:19). In John's Gospel, Jesus says, "I and the Father are one" (John 10:30). The mystery of the fullness of God in the Son in his incarnation is beyond us. Yet this parable depicts a father who leaves the comfort and security of his home and humiliates himself before the village. The coming down and going out to his son is a parable of the incarnation. The costly demonstration of unexpected love in the village street demonstrates a part of the meaning of the cross.

As the father runs through the street, half the village runs after him. The conversation at the edge of the village takes place with a full circle of people standing around them listening. The servants are clearly a part of the crowd, for the father turns to them there in the road. Everything that is said will soon be reported in every home in the village. The father's actions are a drama of reconciliation that can restore the boy to his home and to his community. After this scene, no one in the village can reject or despise him.

A number of orientalisms need explanation. The Greek word for "have compassion" *(splanchizomai)* has as its root "innards" *(splanchnon)*. In the East the Greeks and the Hebrews thought the seat of the emotions was the abdomen. Their perceptions are easy to understand. Whenever a close friend or family member is hurt or even when one thinks about such a potential accident, there is an almost sickening contraction in the abdomen. For the Greeks the abdomen was the seat of the violent passions of anger and lust. The Hebrews, however, understood it to be the center of tender affections, such as kindness and compassion. In villages today the same forms of speech remain. When the villager hears an especially moving story of suffering, he says, "You are cutting up my intestines." Or when a close friend leaves, his companions will say, "Do not cut up our intestines," meaning "We will be deeply hurt by your absence if you leave us." The father sees his son at a distance, before he reaches the edge of the village and knows what the prodigal will suffer from the village as he makes his way through it. The father's "intestines are all cut up in compassion" for his son. Therefore he runs.

Furthermore, the father kisses his son. The word *kissed (katephilēsen)* means either "kissed again and again" or "kissed tenderly." Surely the first meaning is intended. In the Middle East, on occasions of parting as well as reunion, the men of any group are expected to kiss one another. To kiss "tenderly" would be feminine and out of place. But "to kiss again and again" in the robust fashion of men would be the natural expression of deep compassion.

With a little imagination one can easily understand the intense fear the prodigal must have felt as he walked those last few miles to the village. The burning shame of the gauntlet before him would be enough to terrify anyone. But when he arrives, there is an unexpected costly demonstration of his father's love. That love was always there, but he never saw it. Now that love becomes visible and for the first time he is able to understand it.

Islam claims that in this story the boy is saved without a savior. The prodigal returns. The father forgives him. There is no cross, no suffering and no savior. But not so. The incarnation and the atonement are dramatically present in the story and form its first climax. The suffering of the cross was not primarily the physical torture but rather the agony of rejected love. In this parable the father endures such agony all through the estrangement. The very possibility of reconciliation is built on it. The father could have severed his relationship and put his heart at rest by forgetting that he ever had a son. By doing so his suffering would have gradually eased, but at the same time the possibility of the prodigal's return would have vanished.

Any person hurt by evil has two alternatives. One option is to suffer, and through suffering to forgive. The other is to seek revenge. Vengeance avoids suffering. A village proverb says, "He could not beat the donkey, so he beat the saddle." The story behind the proverb tells of a man riding his donkey. The donkey begins galloping out of control, and the man with his saddle is thrown to the ground. Cursing, he runs after the donkey stick in hand but is not able to catch it. He then returns and vents his wrath by beating the saddle. So men and women often seek revenge on the source of their suffering. If it is not available, they turn to a substitute—any substitute.

In the Ethiopian highlands the villagers tell a vivid story with the same moral. In the forest the elephant inadvertently steps on the leopard's son and kills him. The leopard wants revenge. He gathers his leopard friends together to see what they might do.

"Who has killed the leopard's son?" one leopard asks. There is no reply. They are afraid to say, "The elephant." Finally a young leopard stands up and shouts, "The goats! The goats have killed the leopard's son! It is the evil, vengeful goats! They must pay for their crime." At once the leopards take up the cry, swarm out of the forest and slaughter a hundred goats in revenge for the death of the leopard's son.

The father's suffering at the beginning of their estrangement has no effect on the prodigal. He is not even aware of it. A demonstration of the father's suffering for him must be witnessed by the son. Without this the son in his callousness will never discover the suffering of his father and will never understand that he is its cause. Without this visible demonstration the prodigal will return to the house as a servant. Quite likely he will gradually take on more and more of the characteristics of his older son. Without this visible demonstration of costly love, there can be no reconciliation. Isn't this the story of the way of God as he deals with the sin of the world on Golgotha? How will the prodigal respond to this outpouring of costly love?

And the son said to him, "Father, I have sinned against heaven
and before you; I am no longer worthy to be called your son." (Verse 21)

Stunned beyond belief, the prodigal changes his mind and does not finish his speech! The offer to become a craftsman is deliberately set aside. He does not presume to offer any solution to their estrangement! Rather, overwhelmed, he can only put himself completely at the mercy of his father and say, "I am no longer worthy to be called your son." His surrender to his father's will is complete. At the beginning of the story he insisted on unhampered control over his own life. Now he leaves his destiny entirely in his father's hands. He is overwhelmed by this unexpected outpouring of costly love. Words originally composed to manipulate are transformed into a speech of genuine repentance.

Traditional Western interpretation has said that the father interrupted the son and didn't give him a chance to finish his speech. Rather, faced with this incredible event he is flooded with the awareness that his real sin is not the lost money but rather the wounded heart. The reality and enormity of his sin and the resulting intensity of his father's suffering overwhelm him. In a flash of awareness he now knows that there is nothing he can do to make up for what he has done. His proposed offer to work as a servant now seems blasphemous. He is not interrupted. He changes his mind and accepts being found. In this manner he fulfills the definition of repentance that Jesus sets forth in the parable of the lost sheep. Like the lost sheep, the prodigal now accepts to be found.

When the father observes that the son has no bright ideas as to how he, the son, is going to solve the problem of their broken relationship, the father orders a party as did the shepherd and the women.

But the father said to his servants, "Bring quickly the best robe,
and put it on him; and put a ring on his hand, and shoes on his feet;
and bring the fatted calf and kill it, and let us eat and make merry;
for this my son was dead, and is alive again; he was lost, and is found."
And they began to make merry. (Verses 22-24)

The servants are there on the road with the father. The father turns to them and orders them to dress the boy as a son. He doesn't say to the boy, "Go, clean up, shave, and get some decent clothes on." Rather he orders the servants to bring the best robe and dress him. They are to honor him as a son of the house.

The "best robe" is naturally the father's finest robe. In the story of Esther, Haman is asked what he thinks the king should do for the man the king wishes to honor. His first suggestion is to have him dressed in royal robes the king has worn (Esther 6:1-9). The prodigal will attend the banquet attired in his father's most elegant robe. The guests that night will recognize the robe and treat him in a respectful manner because of the clothes he is wearing. They will understand that he has been fully restored to sonship.

The ring is most likely the signet ring of the house. Joseph was also given robes and a ring by Pharaoh (Genesis 41:41-42). From early records we know that the word used here *(daktylios)* refers to a signet ring. In one case it refers to the sealing of a marriage contract, in another the sealing of a will.[1] The Old Testament has many examples of signet rings.[2] Villagers today still sign official documents with a family signet ring. Giving the prodigal a signet ring will be particularly galling to his older brother because this means that the prodigal is trusted with this seal. The rest of the estate is promised to the older son. What will the prodigal do with the power of this ring?

To have shoes on his feet may also be a symbol of his new rank. Slaves go barefoot. Sons wear shoes.

The prodigal's community there in the village is made up of a number of different groups. He will have relations with the family, the family servants and workers, the villagers, and the village elders. The father very carefully reestablishes the boy's broken relationships with each group in turn. Through self-emptying love he restores the prodigal to the family. He orders the servants to "dress him." Thus the servants know they must treat him with respect as a master. The initial welcome was public. Thus the son is restored to the village at large. At the banquet the prodigal wears his

---

[1]James Hope Moulton and George Milligan, *The Vocabulary of the Greek Testament* (Grand Rapids: Eerdmans, 1963), p. 136.

[2]In the Greek Old Testament (LXX) the same word *(daktylios)* more than thirty times translates the Hebrew *tabbaath,* which means "seal" or "signet ring," and is from the root *taba,* "to impress."

father's most expensive robe. The village elders will all thereby accept him out of loyalty to the father. As yet there is no plan for mending one final broken relationship. It will be the hardest of all to mend. His brother is still in the field! When he arrives, he may or may not be pleased with what has taken place.

Only the father is able to restore, and restoration is through grace alone. The younger son brings nothing home but a handful of filthy rags.[3] The Pharisees were complaining that Jesus accepted sinners and ate with them. Jesus doesn't apologize in a patronizing way and say, "After all, they're unfortunate people. Isn't it our duty to show them some kind of fellowship?" Rather, he throws out a challenge. He not only accepts them—he runs to restore them with open arms! He not only eats with them—when they accept his love, he kills the fatted calf in celebration of the success of his costly efforts at reconciliation.

The "fatted calf" that is killed for the banquet is really a "prime beef." The word *fatted (siteuton)* is from the word "grain" *(sitos)*. The "fatted calf" is thus a grain-fed animal with high-quality meat. Meat is a rare delicacy in the village. The father is making a public statement about how joyful he is that he has found his lost son and brought him from death to life.

The son now faces the temptation to indulge in false humility. He can easily refuse sonship, insisting that he is unworthy, and demand servanthood. To do so would be to insist on continuing to live in his spiritual far country. He overcomes this last temptation and in genuine humility accepts restoration, knowing that he is totally unworthy. Everything he has is due to his father's love and bounty.

With the stirring events of this great day of reconciliation as a background, what can be expected from the prodigal in the future? It is easy to assume that he will serve his father with a glad and willing heart. After what has happened he will not serve out of fear of punishment nor will he labor in hope of rewards. Imagine a conversation between the son and some stranger in the field. As the son labors long beyond the call of duty, someone says to him, "Why are you trying to impress your father? What do you want from him now?" He replies in anger, "You have not heard my story! If you had, you wouldn't talk that way!" We can see implicit in this parable the right attitude and motivation for Christian service. Fear of pun-

---

[3]This is reminiscent of Is 64:6.

ishment and desire for rewards are motives that have no place in the heart of a son reconciled to his father by the father's self-emptying love.

A number of modern versions have the Father say, "For this my son was dead and is alive again; he was lost and is found." The word *again* is not essential to the translation.[4] Certainly the father is primarily referring to the recent reconciliation. However, the words used allow us to assume that the father is also referring to his son from the time long before he left home. For indeed the boy was lost and dead to his father's fellowship from the beginning of their estrangement. Now for the first time he is found and brought to life. Had he not been "lost and dead" from the start, he would never have made his cruel request, sold his portion and left home. The older son is still "lost and dead." The father will have to suffer for him as well. Now that the younger son is home, let's stop to summarize his "pilgrim's progress." A series of specific steps can be noted. Granted, no order can give the true picture. Many of these things happen at once. Yet the following movements can be distinguished.

The Path of the Prodigal's Pilgrimage

1. All during the prodigal's absence, the father continues to endure the agony of rejected love.
2. The son comes to the end of his resources and decides to return to his father's house and seek job training and employment.
3. He starts back, hoping yet to save himself.
4. The father demonstrates unexpected love in self-emptying humiliation.
5. Shattered, the son surrenders completely and offers no alternative for their ongoing relationship.
6. The son confesses personal unworthiness.
7. The father offers reconciliation and sonship.
8. The son accepts his father's offer in genuine humility, knowing that all is a gift of pure grace.
9. The son accepts (we can presume) the responsibility of sonship with a new heart. Now he knows, accepts and can return his father's love. Ser-

---

[4]The word for "he is alive" is *ezēsen* as in v. 32. Only here in v. 24 the prefix *ana* is affixed. The connotation of "again" is possible, but in Rom 7:9 and elsewhere the emphasis on "again" is clearly lost and the word becomes merely a synonym of *zaō*. In all of the nearly two thousand years of Syriac and Arabic translations of this text, the word "again" has never appeared.

vice is not now a means to gain more but rather an opportunity accepted joyously to express love and thanks.

10. He enters the family and accepts living with and loving his unlovely brother.

At this juncture the chapter sweeps majestically to its missing conclusion.

CHAPTER FIVE

The Missing Climax

The Arabic for "Behold, I" is repeated at the bottom of the drawing and becomes an outer frame that encompasses the rest of the sentence. Everything this older son says and does is within the big *I*.

His father stands in the courtyard pleading with him to break out of the heavy lines of the big *I*. Does the father succeed? The climax of the story is missing.

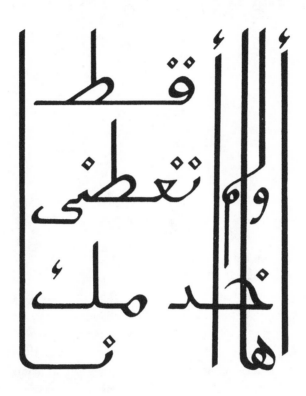

وكم خدمتها أقط تعطني ملك

Gave Me Anything
And You Never
Have Served You

5

The Missing Climax

LUKE 15:25-32

*Now his elder son was in the field; and as he came and drew near
to the house, he heard music and dancing. (Verse 25)*

The family is clearly reasonably wealthy. They own property, for there is an
inheritance to be divided. They have a "prime beef" calf they are feeding in
readiness for any important event that would call for a great banquet. Their
home is large enough to host a crowd that can consume a calf. Furthermore,
they own slaves, hire craftsmen, own festive robes and have goats available
for meals. All of this means that the older son has not been doing farm work
in the fields. No landowner with servants ever engages in manual labor, neither do his sons. The older son has been seated respectably in the shade
somewhere, supervising the laborers. The day is over, and he is on his way
back to the house.

The word *elder* in Greek *(presbyteros)* is the same word used as a title for
the elders of the people, mentioned usually in connection with the scribes.
There is no mistaking who this son represents.

As he approaches the house, he hears music and dancing. The word
music (symphōnias) can mean a band or a single instrument. In all prob-
ability there would have been two or three instruments including a drum
and a stringed instrument of some type. The elder son would have heard
the drum at a distance, and its rhythm would have told him that some
kind of a joyful gathering was in progress. The *dancing (chorōn)* probably
means a band of singers and dancers. The word also carries the possible
meaning of a "circular dance." One of the most ancient dances in the

world is the circular stick dance of Middle Eastern peasants. It is simple and graceful. Almost every villager knows it. The same word for "dancing" appears in the Greek version of the Old Testament in Psalm 149:3 ("Let them praise his name with dancing") and Psalm 150:4 ("Praise him with timbrel and dance"). And although a different word is used, David also danced before the Lord when the sacred ark was brought up to Jerusalem (2 Samuel 6:14).

Confusion and excitement reign hand in hand in village life. Order is considered dull, but there is no order here! We can easily visualize the scene. The principal guests have arrived, because the music and dancing have begun. A large crowd is mingling, and there is much laughing and clapping to the rhythm of the drum. Doors and windows are wide open, and a great time is being had by all. Every few minutes one of the women breaks out in a loud, shrill "joy cry" that intensifies the excitement all around. A group of young boys is milling around in the courtyard of the house. They are not old enough to join the banquet, but can enjoy the music and excitement from outside the house.

As he approaches the house and hears the music, the natural reaction for the older son would be that of pleasure in anticipation of a delightful evening with the leading men of the village. One expects him to enter the house with no more ado. Inside the house his father can tell him what the banquet is all about! Instead he stands aloof.

And he called one of the young boys and asked what this meant.
(Verse 26)

The word translated as "servant" *(pais)* in the RSV (and NIV) can be translated "son," "young boy" or "servant." Clearly "son" does not fit. The choice is between "young boy" and "servant."

Pais means "young boy" in a number of key New Testament passages. Herod kills all the male children *(paidas)* in Bethlehem (Matthew 2:16). Jesus cast a demon out of a young boy *(pais,* Matthew 17:18). The boy *(pais)* Jesus stayed behind in the temple at the age of twelve (Luke 2:43). "Servant" is possible,[1] but not likely because the servants are all busy with the meal inside the house. However, the crowd of young boys, mentioned above, will

---

[1]Mt 8:6, 8, 13; 12:18; 14:2; Lk 1:54, 69; 7:7; Acts 4:25. But Luke uses the word *doulos* for "servant" twenty-seven times. Thus *doulos,* rather than *pais,* is his most common word for servant.

be milling around in the courtyard. It is a young boy that the older son naturally approaches.[2]

These young boys comprise part of the anticipated crowd the prodigal feared as he made his way home. With no boys' club, school program or organized sports, any special gathering will attract the gang. If a dramatic event, such as they have already witnessed, is to culminate in a banquet, they most certainly will be there. They are not invited to the banquet itself but will mill around in the courtyard, joining in the laughter, perhaps clapping in rhythm with the drum and gyrating in their own dances. With great excitement they will tell each newcomer about the speeches they heard on the road. They become a conglomerate mass of young humanity that is a part of village life at any focus of excitement. As the older son approaches the house, it would be natural for him to summon a young boy out of this crowd and ask what all this means. Significantly the Arabic Bible versions across the centuries have always translated this word as "young boy" not "servant."

> *And he said to him, "Your brother has come, and your father has killed the fatted calf, because he has received him with peace." (Verse 27)*

This young boy is the "Greek chorus" of the play. He tells the audience what is really happening in the drama. The essential parts of his speech are given with brevity. The young boy does not offer a personal opinion, he represents what the town is saying about the occasion. He refers to the father as "your father." Were he a servant, he would have said, "my master."

The young boy's speech is freighted with meaning. He tells the older son that the father has received a sinner and is in process of sitting down and eating with him. This is precisely the complaint of the Pharisees against Jesus (Luke 15:2). Thus by this point in the story it is unmistakably clear that the figure of the father has evolved into a symbol for Jesus himself. But there is more.

The young boy does not say, "Your brother has *returned*." "Return" is a big word in the Bible. In Isaiah, God says regarding the wicked person, "Let him *return* to the LORD that he may have mercy on him" (Is 55:7). Indeed in Hebrew the word "return" and the word "repent" are the same word *(shub)*.

---

[2]In the play, I have turned this young boy into a servant for dramatic, not exegetical, reasons.

Here in the parable the young boy tells the older son, "Your brother has *hēkei.*" In Greek *hēko* can mean "has arrived"; it can also mean "is here." There is no hint of the prodigal having made a journey of repentance and return. Rather, he has simply appeared and only then did things start to happen.

Furthermore, the father has received the prodigal *hygiainō*. As a Greek word, used within Greek culture, *hygiainō* has to do with good health, and the English word *hygiene* is derived from it. But every occurrence of *hygiainō* in the Greek Old Testament translates the great Hebrew word *shalom* (peace). When a Greek speaking Jew heard the word *hygiainō* he or she thought *shalom*. *Shalom* includes good health, but it also means "reconciliation." Without doubt this Hebrew word was on the lips of Jesus in his original telling of this story. If the older son had been told "your father has received your brother *safe and sound*" (as in the RSV and NIV), the older son would have rushed at once into the banquet because such a report would have meant that the father had not yet decided what to do with the prodigal. The older son would naturally want to be present to insist, "Make the irresponsible fool get a job and return the money before you let him in the door!" But if the father has already received the prodigal "with peace" then the two of them are reconciled—and the older son's point of view has already lost. This explains the older son's explosive wrath. What then will he do with his anger?

> *But he was angry and refused to go in.*
> *His father came out and entreated him. (Verse 28)*

Everything left in the house is legally the property of the older son. Although the father still maintains authority, the remaining wealth is pledged to the older son. At the death of the father the older son will acquire the right of disposition. The father can spend the usufruct (the profits) of the estate as he sees fit. But if they are not spent, they are added to the capital that the older son will one day inherit. Giving a sumptuous banquet is fully within the rights of the father, and the older son can say nothing. But he is not pleased because these profits of the estate would be added to the capital if they were not spent. One day that capital would be his.

But there is something else. At such a banquet the father sits with the guests. The older son often stands and serves the meal as a "head waiter." The important difference between him and the other servants is that he joins in conversation with the seated company. By stationing the older son as a kind of hovering head waiter, the family is in effect saying, "You, our guests, are so great that our son is your servant." But can he bring himself to serve his brother?

The younger son has been reinstated through costly grace that is in violation of traditional village honor. The older son can easily feel that the father has dishonored the family in the eyes of the community. Reconciliation and restoration without a penalty paid by the offender is too much for him to understand or accept. For certain types of people, grace is not only amazing, it is also infuriating.[3]

The older son's response is crucially significant. He refuses to enter the banquet hall where the guests have already arrived. In any social situation, banquet or no banquet, the male members of the family must come and shake hands with the guests even if they don't stay and visit. They cannot stay aloof if they are anywhere in the vicinity of the house. Failure to fulfill this courtesy is a personal insult to the guests and to the father, as host. The older son knows this and thereby his action is an intentional public insult to his father.

A similar situation takes place in the story of Esther. King Ahasuerus summons Queen Vashti to appear at a banquet, and she refuses with dire results. We are told, "The king was enraged, and his anger burned within him." The wise men of the kingdom quickly arrive at the conclusion that her action is a threat to all of them, and she is deposed with dispatch (Esther 1). In the banquet under consideration we fully expect similar anger to burn within the father.

Word of the son's refusal reaches his father immediately and spreads to all the guests. Nothing is secret in a village. This is an open rupture of relationship between the son and his father. The situation is very serious because all this takes place publicly during a banquet. Because it is in public, this rebellion of the older son is more serious than the earlier rebellion of the prodigal. Everyone in the banquet hall tenses expectantly, awaiting the father's reaction. They assume the older son will be punished immediately or ignored until the guests are gone and then dealt with harshly.

For the second time in the same day the father's response is incredible. Once again he demonstrates a willingness to endure shame and self-emptying love in order to reconcile. The parable briefly and succinctly states, "His

---

[3]The same irritation appears in the parable of the generous vineyard owner in Mt 20:1-16.

father came out and entreated him." It is almost impossible to convey the shock that must have reverberated through the banquet hall when the father deliberately left his guests, humiliated himself before all, and went out in the courtyard to try to reconcile his older son.

The father loves both of his sons indiscriminately. He gives of himself equally for both of them irrespective of their actions. The same self-emptying sacrificial love is demonstrated visibly and dramatically on the same day in similar ways for two different sons with different kinds of needs.

He goes out to *entreat,* not to punish or condemn. The Greek word for "call" is *kaleō*. Many different shades of meaning can be given to the word by prefixing prepositions to it. For example:

en-kaleō: "call against" or "accuse"

eis-kaleō: "call in" or "invite"

epi-kaleō: "call by name"

pro-kaleō: "provoke" or "challenge"

pros-kaleō: "summon" or "call to oneself" as an officer would summon an orderly or a master a servant

syn-kaleō: "call together"

para-kaleō: "appeal to" or "entreat" or "try to reconcile"

Luke knows this family of words well and uses it more than any other New Testament writer. In verse 26 the older son "summons" *(pros-kaleō)* the youth to demand information. Here in verse 28 we fully expect the father to likewise "summon" *(pros-kaleō)* his older son, to demand an explanation for his public rudeness. Or perhaps he will "challenge" him *(pro-kaleō)* or even "accuse" him *(en-kaleō)*. Instead, in direct contrast to the son who summons an inferior to demand an explanation, the father goes out to "entreat" *(para-kaleō)*, to "appeal to," to "try to reconcile." Robertson, in his monumental grammar, gives us the key to the two prepositions used here with the same word. He says that *para* merely means "beside" or "alongside" (cf. our *parallel*), and *pros* suggests "facing one another."[4] So the son "summons" the youth to stand facing him as an inferior should. But the father tries to "en-

---

[4]A. T. Robertson, *A Grammar of the Greek New Testament in the Light of Historical Research* (Nashville: Broadman, 1934), p. 613.

treat" his son. He calls on him to "stand alongside" his father, to look at the world from the father's perspective. Paul uses this same word in 2 Corinthians 5:20: "We beseech *[para-kaleō]* you on behalf of Christ, be reconciled to God." Amazingly this same kind of beseeching is the course of action the father chooses in the face of his angry and rebellious son.

The father's agony of rejected love is more keenly felt with the older son because of the son's public insult. Earlier in the day the father paid the price of self-emptying love in order to reconcile the prodigal to himself. Now he must pay the same price to try to win the older son. The father must go out to his boy in humiliation if he wants a son. If he is satisfied with a servant, self-emptying suffering is unnecessary. He can have the older son dragged in, tied up and later punished. But this will cause greater bitterness and deeper estrangement. If he overlooks the incident, he is finished as a father. The son's next move would be even more threatening to the father's authority. The father does the only thing that can open the door to genuine repentance and restoration. He pays the price of reconciliation. Once again incarnation and atonement meet.

> *But he answered his father, "Lo, these many years I have served you,*
> *and I never disobeyed your command; yet you never*
> *gave me a kid, that I might make merry with my friends.*
> *But when this son of yours came, who has devoured your living with harlots,*
> *you killed for him the fatted calf!" (Verses 29-30)*

The older son is clearly condemned out of his own mouth. His whole being suddenly comes to focus in this brief speech. Many things are evident and warrant attention.

1. The son refuses to participate in reconciling his brother to the village. The woman, the shepherd and the father, each in their separate ways, made the necessary effort to recover that which was lost. They labored, indeed suffered, in order to find. But the older son makes no such effort and accepts no such responsibility.

2. He rebels against his father. In this speech he insults his father for the second time in one evening by omitting any title. The phrase "O father" is an essential sign of respect. The older son chooses to be rude. The younger son was a rebel and knew it. His brother is a rebel and does not know it. He answers, "I have never disobeyed you."

3. He has broken a relationship, not a law. The law he fulfills to the letter as he proudly affirms. Like his brother, he now breaks his father's heart.

4. He accuses his father of favoritism by saying, "You never gave me a *kid,* that I might make merry with my friends." That is—he gets a calf, I don't even get a goat!

5. He reads himself out of the family. Clearly his brother and his father are not among his friends with whom he wishes to make merry!

6. He refuses partnership with his father. His request has the same tone as the earlier request of his brother: "I want mine!" His goal seems to be to get from his father, not share with his father. The older son has his portion. It is the lack of unrestricted authority over it that he resents.

7. He despises his brother. Unwilling to call him "my brother," he refers to him as "your son." Also he gives a fabricated account of his brother's actions. The older son has clearly just come in from the field and knows nothing, yet he accuses his brother of living with harlots. He refuses to welcome his brother home or to be reconciled to him. He will not rejoice and will not participate in serving a banquet where his brother is seated.

8. He catches himself in an unsuspected trap. He says that the younger brother devoured "your living with harlots." Thereby he refuses to acknowledge that the portion given by the father to the son was really the prodigal's to do with as he pleased. Yet in the same breath he is whining that he, the elder son, does not have full freedom to do what he wants with his portion.

9. He understands his relationship to his father as that of a servant before his master. He says, "All these years I have served you," and like a servant he begins demanding his rights. He, the hard worker, doesn't even get a kid, and the lazy prodigal gets a grain-fed calf! How monstrously unjust!!! A servant obeys the law. A son responds to love. His choice is law, and his concern is rewards.

10. The older son needs to be forgiven by his father and his brother. He thinks they must apologize to him, but in reality he needs their forgiveness. The older son's unwillingness to be reconciled to his brother forces him to break fellowship with his father. Jesus makes the same point in the Lord's Prayer. In this parable the reason behind it becomes clear. The man who cannot live with his brother obviously cannot live within the family fellowship; thereby harmony with his father is impossible. The parallels between the two sons continue to multiply.

11. He falsifies the meaning of the banquet. The young boy tells him that

the banquet is in celebration of the father's success in creating *shalom*. The older son cries out, "you killed for him the fatted calf." The banquet is in honor of the father not the brother. The older son does not allow himself to understand this.

12. He is consumed with envy, pride, bitterness, sarcasm, anger, resentment, self-centeredness, hate, stinginess, self-satisfaction and self-deception. Yet he appears to see his actions as a righteous search for honor.

This dialogue, like the earlier interchange with the prodigal on the road, does not take place in private. As the father goes out, a number of servants, some of the lesser guests and a throng of unidentified bystanders all go out with him. They, with the inevitable gang of young boys, are all in a circle listening. I have the distinct impression that the older son is playing to the grandstand. He knows his speech will be repeated almost word for word in every home. He wants to make his position crystal clear. He succeeds!

> *And he said to him, "Son, you are always with me, and all that*
> *is mine is yours. It was fitting to make merry and be glad,*
> *for this your brother was dead, and is alive; he was lost, and is found."*
> *(Verse 31-32)*

If the father is an oriental patriarch, he will cry out, "Enough! Lock him up! I will deal with him later!" By contrast, this father bypasses the omission of a title and overlooks the bitterness, the arrogance, the distortion of fact and the accusation of favoritism. There is no judgment, no criticism and no rejection. He opens his reply with *teknon*, which is not the ordinary word for "son" *(huios)*. *Huios* is used for son in verses 11, 13, 19, 21, 24, 25 and 30. The new word *(teknon)* introduced here is a special word for "son" indicating love and affection. It is the word Mary uses when Jesus is found in the temple and she says, "Son, why have you treated us so?" (Luke 2:48). The father did not use this especially affectionate title when telling the servants to dress the younger son, but he uses it here. It can be translated "My dear son!" Very gently he corrects only one point of the son's speech as he reminds him that the prodigal is "your brother." The rest of the speech is a defense of joy.

The shepherd felt no need to explain to his neighbors why he was happy when he found his sheep, and the women did not have to argue to convince her friends that they should rejoice with her over finding her coin. Yet this is what the father is forced to do! How sad and unnatural the Pharisees' complaint in verse 1 becomes when it appears in this story of stories!

The parable of the prodigal son is unfinished. Jesus leaves the account in midair. The entire trilogy moves to its poignant climax in the courtyard. Inside the banquet hall tense guests wait to see if the son will give up his rebellion and enter the house in humility. But the ending is missing. Clearly it is omitted on purpose. Jesus' reason for this omission is obvious in that he is addressing the group of religious sinners who stand in opposition to his message. There is still a chance for them to be reconciled to the Father, present among them in Jesus' person. In hardness of heart they can also reject his love and increase his suffering. The story unfolds in history with, "Then the older son in great anger took his stick and struck his father." Is not the end of the story the cross?[5] But another option is still open.

By this point in the story Jesus is on stage in the person of the father. The Pharisees are on stage in the person of the older son. Jesus is telling them, "This is my explanation of why I sit and eat with sinners. What now are you going to do with me?" Each reader or listener is pressed to ponder the same question.

A parable is not a delivery system for an idea. It is not like a shell casing that can be discarded once the idea (the shell) is fired. Rather a parable is a house in which the reader or listener is invited to take up residence. The reader is encouraged to look out on the world from the point of view of the story. A "house" has a variety of windows and rooms. Thus the parable may have one primary idea with other secondary ideas encased within it. It may have a cluster of theological themes held together by the story. Naturally the interpreter should only look for the themes that were available to the first-century audience listening to Jesus. What themes are set forth in this marvelous "Gospel within the Gospel" as it has been called for centuries?

We are almost embarrassed with riches but I would suggest the following.

The Parable of the Two Lost Sons— the Theological Cluster

Sin. The parable exhibits two types of sin. One is the sin of the law-breaker and the other the sin of the law-keeper. Each centers on a broken relationship. One breaks that relationship while failing to fulfill the expectations of

---

[5]Granted, in the Synoptic Gospels the Pharisees do not participate in the event of the cross. The temple authorities with the cooperation of Pilate are responsible. Yet the Pharisees inflict on him the pain of rejection as they oppose his person and message.

the family and society. The second breaks his relationship while fulfilling those same expectations.

Freedom. God grants ultimate freedom to humankind, which is the freedom to reject his love. Humankind is free to choose its own way even if that way causes infinite pain to the loving heart of God.

Repentance. Two types of repentance are dramatically illustrated: (1) earn your acceptance as a servant/craftsman, (2) accept the costly gift of being found as a son/daughter.

Grace. Grace is a freely offered love that seeks and suffers in order to save.

Joy. For the father, joy is in finding. For the son, joy is in being found and restored to community.

Fatherhood. The image of God as a compassionate father is here given its finest definition in all of Scripture. That definition includes the offer of costly love to law-breakers and to law-keepers.

Sonship. Each son returns to the father either defining (the older son) or intending to define (the prodigal) his relationship to the father as that of a servant before a master. The father will not accept this definition. He offers costly love to each, out of his determination to have sons responding to love rather than merely servants obeying commands.

Christology. Twice the father takes upon himself the form of a suffering servant who in each case offers a costly demonstration of unexpected love. The woman and the shepherd do some of the same on a lesser scale. There is dramatic "self-emptying" in each case. The third parable embodies an implied one-to-one relationship between the actions of Jesus and the actions of the father in that each welcomes sinners into table fellowship. This unity of action affirms a unity of person.

Family/community. The father offers costly love to his sons in order to restore them to fellowship in the context of a family or community. The family is Jesus' metaphor for the church.

Incarnation and atonement. The father empties himself and goes down and out to meet the sons where they are (incarnation). In the process he demonstrates costly redeeming love (atonement). Because of who he is, these acts generate incalculable atoning power. Some of the deepest levels of the meaning of both the incarnation and the cross are clearly exposed.

Eucharist. As he partakes in the banquet the prodigal is sitting and eating with the father who through self-giving love won the prodigal into fellowship with himself. Thus the heart of the Eucharist is clearly affirmed. The mood of the banquet/Eucharist is that of a celebration, not a funeral. The price paid by the shepherd, the woman and the father are not forgotten at the banquets that conclude each parable. But the atmosphere at the banquet is that of joy at the success of the costly efforts expended in finding the lost.

Eschatology. The messianic banquet has begun. All who accept the father's costly love are welcome as his guests. Table fellowship with Jesus is a proleptic celebration of the messianic banquet of the end times. The parable of the great banquet in Luke 14:15-24 precedes this parable. Luke's Gospel presents the reader with the former parable where "to eat bread in the kingdom of God" finally means to accept table fellowship with Jesus. This same theme is woven into this parable as well.[6]

The above is an attempt to clarify the theological content of the parable. But what of its emotional impact? In the following play I have tried to present some of these ideas in dramatic form. I hope that it will prove useful in communicating at least a part of the richness of this story when we place it within the world of Middle Eastern traditional life.

---

[6]Revised from Kenneth E. Bailey, *Jacob and the Prodigal* (Downers Grove, Ill.: InterVarsity Press, 2003), pp. 115-17.

The design around the title says, "And he said, 'A certain man had two sons.'"

The older son (the characters on the left) seems to have a tenuous hold within the house, but in reality he too stands outside.

Both sons are equally present from the first.

PART TWO

"Two Sons Have I Not"

A ONE-ACT PLAY IN
FOUR SCENES

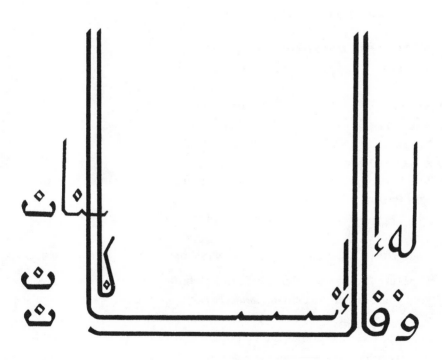

Introduction

This play is an attempt to read between the lines of the story of the prodigal son. I have tried to add detail with a sanctified imagination, reading in only that which will both be faithful to traditional Middle Eastern village life and will illuminate the theological and emotional content of the parable.

Cast requirements: eight actors/readers
Time: early in the first century
Place: a small Galilean village

The Cast in the Order of Appearance

SHALUK:	The family head steward (male or female)
OBED:	The younger son
ADAM:	The older son
ABU-ADAM:	The father
SERGIS:	A Greek pig herder
ANTIPAS OR ATHENA:	Sergis's son or daughter.
THE MAYOR:	Mayor of the home village (man or woman)
THE PRIEST:	Leader of the local synagogue. His title is "Abuna," which means "our father"

Most of the characters have some symbolic meaning. These are as follows:

SHALUK: This person's name is from a Hebrew word that means "messenger." The Greek translation *apostolos,* became our English *apostle.* He or she is a person of great stature, who shares the confidences of both the father and Obed. He or she has served faithfully for many years and is perhaps fifty years old.

OBED: This young man is anxious to live life to the fullest and is quite sure he understands all that this means. At the beginning he is defiant and rebellious. In scene two he is shaken and subdued. The light dawns in scene three. His name is from a Hebrew root meaning "to be lost" (ʾ*bd*). He is lost to all around him and to himself until he sees the unexpected outpouring of his father's love.

ADAM: The older son symbolizes proud self-righteousness. As a religious sinner he is rebellious within the law. Confident of the righteousness of all he does, he is sure of his opinions—all of them. Young and hard, he is the first Adam.

ABU-ADAM: In the house the father is a symbol for God, and later in the play he becomes a symbol of God in Christ. "Abu-Adam" means "the father of Adam." In him holiness and love fuse. Righteousness and justice are brought together. Anyone playing this part should prepare himself by reading the first essay in P. T. Forsyth's little classic *God the Holy Father* (Naperville, Ill.: Allenson, 1957). There should be no deep-voiced, slow-moving, stylized acting so often used in this connection. The father is a real person. The key to understanding him is that he knows from the beginning what he must do. He debates with full vigor but with the sense of a person who is going over old ground. He never has the sense of "I never thought of that before." He tries earnestly to get his friends to see that a radical solution is necessary for a deep-seated problem. He is able to combine great firmness and great compassion. His lines with his older son should reflect this combination.

SERGIS: The Greek shepherd and his son or daughter are not symbolic of anything. This man is simply a crude Greek peasant with a built-in distaste for the local Semitic population. He has immigrated from poverty-stricken Greece, yet feels himself superior because he is Greek.

ANTIPAS (or ATHENA): This character is a few years younger than Obed. He (or she) was awestruck when Obed came to town and is genuinely sorry for him. They have had a number of months together, and Antipas (or Athena) has come to genuinely like Obed and wants to help him if he (or she) can.

THE MAYOR: The mayor symbolizes justice defined as observance of law. There is the ring of authority in the mayor's voice and he (or she) is accustomed to obedience. Discipline and order are the mayor's specialties and he (or she) understands their importance. As a straightforward, practical person, the mayor misses many of the subtleties of the debate. The mayor is responsible for order in the village and is at first supremely confident that the father's problem can be solved by punishment. Broken law demands it. The mayor is rather badly shaken when faced with a type of rebellion that cannot be overcome by punishment. He (or she) has a big voice but doesn't need to use it. (In a traditional village setting the mayor would be a man. I see no reason why a woman should not play this part today even if it does not fit the original world of the parable.)

THE PRIEST: The priest symbolizes love and mercy. He too holds a position of influence in the community. He is highly respected and knows that mercy, love, and forgiveness run all through the history of God's dealings with his people. As the problem of Adam's rebellion presents itself, he knows that love and forgiveness must be shown, but he has no idea what is really involved in showing them. He is shattered when he sees the price that must be paid. He does not understand the real meaning of forgiveness, and thus his thinking, like the mayor's, is incomplete. He is middle-aged and speaks slowly and sympathetically.

Scene One

The Breakfast Table

The father takes an unprecedented step. He divides his living between his two sons. Both sons get their share. This ten-word sentence is only three words in Arabic. "His living" is split by the word "between the two of them." The intruding black lines symbolize the two sons who have not only split the father's living but also his heart.

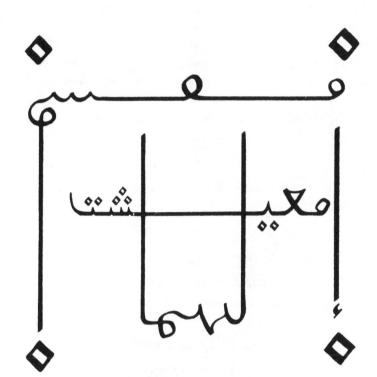

And He Divided His Living
Between the Two of Them

Scene One

Time: 8:00 in the morning about A.D. 15.

Place: The dining-reception room in the house of a leading family in a small Galilean village.

As the lights go up, Obed is sitting tense and motionless, facing the audience from behind a dining table slightly left of stage center. The table is rectangular and seats six. On it are a pitcher and an overturned glass. A chair lies overturned to the right of the table. A closet for clothes and a cupboard for food and dishes stand against the upstage wall. Shaluk enters from a door at stage left. Seeing Obed, he purses his lips and gives out a deep sigh. He shakes his head, notices the chair, crosses the stage and picks it up, setting it in place at the end of the table. He picks up the glass, pours water into it and sets it before Obed.

SHALUK: Well! Are you proud of yourself for having sat there all night?

OBED: *(angry and irritated)* I wasn't sleepy.

SHALUK: You may not be sleepy, but you are so bone tired I don't think you even know whether it is night or day.

OBED: *(defiantly)* So far it has been night! But day is about to dawn!

SHALUK: *(frustrated)* Oh, if that were only true! If you go through with it, Obed, you will be blowing out the only flicker of light you have left.

OBED: What do you mean—*if* I go through with it?

SHALUK: *(Goes to cupboard upstage from door on stage left. All through the scene he is busy getting out two more glasses, three plates, a bowl of beans, a large loaf of bread and a plate of cheese, and arranging them on the table. The bread he places in a prominent position in the center of the table.)* So you are determined.

OBED: Yes! Determined! Determined to be free!

SHALUK: Again? I don't think you were even listening to me last night! Freedom, Obed, must mean freedom to *be,* not freedom to escape.

OBED: I've heard your old, silly arguments again and again, and I'm sick of them. I suppose you think my brother is free.

SHALUK: *(fiercely)* No, he's not! But I am. I am free to be the man I have always wanted to be. Free to love and be loved. Free to care for others and not merely myself. Free from hatred even of Adam. Free to serve with a holy passion.

OBED: I'm beginning to understand why my father picked you as head steward. I wonder how he browbeat you into believing all that nonsense!

SHALUK: It seems there is no use.

OBED: Well, you worked on me until the third watch of the night last night. Wasn't that enough?

SHALUK: Was it that late?

OBED: It must have been! You ranted on by the hour with all that rubbish of yours about freedom and responsibility and what this would do to my father.

SHALUK: But it will.

OBED: Now look! I don't mean it that way! I don't care when he dies. I just want my rights, that's all.

SHALUK: *(exploding)* You don't care!—Oh, what's the use!

ADAM: *(entering from stage left)* That's right. What's the use? I've been saying that for a long time. Good morning, Shaluk.

SHALUK: Good morning, Adam. *(coldly)* Greet your brother, Adam.

ADAM: My brother? *(sarcastically)* Oh, yes, my brother—I had almost forgotten; it's been so long since he's acted like one. *(mockingly with a deep bow)* Good morning—*brother!*

Obed stares straight ahead and does not flinch.

SHALUK: *(irritated)* Must you? Can't you see he's upset?

ADAM: Well, he ought to be, the way he's been neglecting the work around here!

SHALUK: He's done his best.

ADAM: Really? *(turning to Obed)* How many denarii did you get for that cow in the market yesterday? *(answering his own question)* Oh!

You didn't make it to the market! Unexpectedly held up, no doubt?

Well . . . eh . . . how is the repair work coming on that dry wall down by the crossroads where the goats always get in and eat the green wheat? *(pause)* Oh, you didn't find any workmen to hire. Yes, of course.

Well . . . eh . . . how many bids did you get from different camel drivers to move our chaff from the threshing floor into the courtyard? Oh! Oh, yes, of course! You didn't make it out to ask around the village.

OBED: *(irritated)* Shut up, will you!

ADAM: *(to Shaluk)* He's done his best all right. Yes, as a matter of fact I think you're right Shaluk—I think he has done his best.

OBED: I said, "Shut up"!

ADAM: Now, is that any way to talk to your elder brother, Obed? I don't believe I have said anything but the truth.

OBED: I'm not going to take this any longer! Leave me alone!

ADAM: Well, Father won't keep after you! So somebody has to!

SHALUK: Oh, stop it, both of you! Sit down and eat your breakfast.

ADAM: Good idea! Agreed! *(moves the chair six inches farther away, then sits down beside Obed, who gets up and crosses down left)* What's the matter? I don't have leprosy you know.

SHALUK: For heaven's sake, must we begin every day like this?

Father enters from door on stage right. Everybody freezes.

FATHER: Good morning, sons.

BOTH SONS: Good morning, Father.

FATHER: *(meditatively)* The sunrise was incredibly beautiful this morning. *(places his staff at edge of stage down right behind door)* The air was clear from the rain—so clear I could see the hills of Gilead. The valley was hidden by thick fog, which moved slowly south, covering the forests of Bashan as it moved. The sound of my sandals on the loose rock of the hill and the call of a single circling kite were the only sounds of the morning.

(senses the tension of the room) But . . . say . . . what's going on here?

ADAM: Nothing. I was just reflecting on all the leftover work I expect I'll have to pick up today.

FATHER: No one *has* to do anything in our family, son.

ADAM: Well, when half the work is left undone, sometimes we *have* to do a lot of things.

FATHER: *(patiently)* Not because I demand them, son. All I hope for is a response of love from each of you. *(sits at the table)*

ADAM: *(properly)* Of course, Father!

FATHER: *(quietly)* Obed! Obed!

OBED: Yes, Father.

FATHER: Come and eat with us.

OBED: I'm not hungry.

FATHER: *(very patiently)* Son, come and eat with us.

OBED: *(with rising intensity)* I will not eat in this house again!

FATHER: What do you mean, son?

OBED: What I mean is . . .

SHALUK: *(pleadingly shouts)* Obed!

OBED: What I mean is . . . I . . . I want my portion of the family's wealth!

There is a stunned silence around the room.

ADAM: *(rising slowly)* You want your what?

OBED: Give me my share of the family's wealth.

SHALUK: *(rushing up to the father)* Abu-Adam, the boy is ill! He has not slept all night! He doesn't know what he's saying!

OBED: I know very well what I am saying. It is the law of Moses. I have the right to one third of the family wealth. I want my share!

FATHER: *(amazed)* Yes, my son, of course. You shall have your share—

but in due time—it is our custom . . .

OBED: I want mine—*now!*

ADAM: *(loud and harsh)* Sure, sure . . . now! *Now,* he says! Go ahead and say it. You can't wait for Father to die!

OBED: Why do you always deliberately misunderstand me. All I want is my share of the estate!

ADAM: *(with rising anger all through this series of speeches)* Sure, sure, take it now! Tell the village, tell the whole world that a son of the family of Abu-Adam is anxious for his father to die!

OBED: *(stubbornly)* I want my share!

ADAM: Why not? Your father will not be able to sit again with honor in the gate. The children will mock me in the street.

OBED: I want my share of the estate!

ADAM: The young men will hiss at me as I pass. The village will remember that Obed of the house of Abu-Adam was anxious for his father to die! *(continuing through gritted teeth)* I have endured you and faithfully served my father, but there comes a day when every son must show himself a man! *(rushes over to the door down right, picks up the father's stick, crosses down left to Obed, hooks one leg from under Obed with his leg and spins him to the ground; then turns to his father)* Father, will you beat him? Or must I?

Father with slow movements and great anguish rises, goes over to Adam, snatches the stick from his hand, and raises it above his head. Grabbing it at both ends, in a great dramatic gesture he breaks it in two over his knee.[1]

FATHER: *(with great intensity)* How long? How long? How much more must I suffer before I have a son? *(throws the two pieces of stick on the floor)* Get out, both of you!

Adam stomps out the right door. Obed picks himself up and, rather shaken, exits left.

---

[1]A four-foot stick or dowel can be sawn three-fourths of the way through. This will assure that it will break easily over the knee of the father.

SHALUK: *(approaching the table and nervously adjusting the plates)* I am very sorry, Abu-Adam.

FATHER: Dawn comes after the dark of night Shaluk. We must be patient. *(starts to exit stage left, reaches the door, pauses briefly with his hand on it, then goes out)*

SHALUK: *(advances slowly to the table, sees the loaf of bread, lifts it in the air, and says very intensely)* And so . . . the bread is unbroken!

The lights dim.

Scene Two

The Herd of Swine

The prodigal is leaving home. The Arabic sentence begins at the bottom of the drawing. The first phrase suggests his movements out and away.

The country "far away" is represented by the word at the top. The prodigal is not only moving to a geographically distant place, but culturally he will be in a strange new world where the people keep pigs. In the drawing, gentle curves give way to geometric designs suggesting a Greek city with its "citizens."

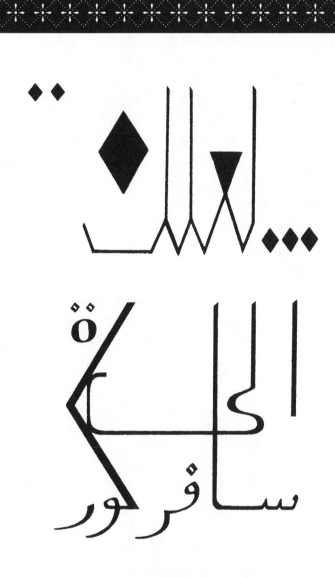

He Traveled into a
Country Far Away

Scene Two

Time: Two months later.

Place: The slope of a hill a few miles north of Antioch, in Syria.

Three pig shepherds are sprawled on the ground. Their herd is on a slope in front of them that rises up over the heads of the audience in our imagination. Obed, in rags and barefoot, lies on his side apparently asleep with his back to the audience. There is an earthenware bowl in front of Sergis.

If Antipas is a female, the lines should be appropriately adjusted.

SERGIS: We'll make it. Don't worry! We'll make it. I'll tell you!—The stories my father used to tell—you surely can remember some of them, Antipas.

ANTIPAS: I was pretty small, Father.

SERGIS: That, mind you, was a real famine!

ANTIPAS: Tell me about it, Father?

SERGIS: Well, Anthony was on the way down. That witch Cleopatra was still trying to make Alexandria greater than Rome. Augustus was on the way up. Then Herod and the Seleucids were all mixed up in the middle.

ANTIPAS: So what happened?

SERGIS: All those different armies ravaged the countryside around here. They didn't leave a thing. Very little was even planted because the men were away at war. Then on top of it all, the rain was bad that year. Besides, even if you did raise a crop, somebody's army would come plundering through and take it away from you.

ANTIPAS: What was that like?

SERGIS: Hell! They ate your food, raped your women, slaughtered your cattle, and burned the doors of your houses for fuel. If a village didn't cooperate, they roughed you up. If you did cooperate, their enemies came through the next week to burn you out for collaborating. You couldn't win!

ANTIPAS: What did you do, Father?

SERGIS: Your grandfather took us to a cave up there in the hills. *(points* *up out over the heads of the audience)*

ANTIPAS: But how did you eat?

SERGIS: *(remembering and shaking his head)* Some of us didn't! Grand-father never told us much. I guess it was too hard even to think about.

ANTIPAS: Why? What happened, Father?

SERGIS: *(gravely)* Your great-uncle Urbanis told me after grandfather died. It seems I had a younger brother and sister. There wasn't enough for all of us, so grandfather made a decision. They fed me; my younger brother and baby sister were left to starve.

OBED: *(in disgust)* In my father's house there is bread enough and to spare, even in time of famine. *(turns over as he talks)*

SERGIS: Well! Our Galilean prince is still alive. I thought perhaps you had died in the night. Look, why don't you break down?

ANTIPAS: He can't, Father!

SERGIS: What do you mean—he can't? Sure he can. *(to Obed)* Look here, son, just try little of this pork. *(gestures, indicating the bowl)* Granted, the brains and the intestines aren't much. But at least it will keep us alive. *(offers him the bowl)*

ANTIPAS: Don't press him, Father. It's all he's got left!

OBED: *(fiercely)* It is forbidden! *(sits up)*

SERGIS: Now let's be reasonable! Your prophet . . . what was his name?

ANTIPAS: Moses.

SERGIS: Yeah, Moses. Was there a famine when Yahweh told Moses to not eat pork?

OBED: *(fiercely)* You must call him *Adonai!*

SERGIS: Oh, all right, all right! Adonai. Don't get so upset! *(under his breath)* Of all the ridiculous . . .

ANTIPAS: It's important to him, Father.

SERGIS: As I was saying, Adonai isn't even god up here in Syria. This isn't his land. He has no power here. Why over in the temple, his name isn't even listed with the other gods.

OBED: *(angry and defiant)* He is the Lord of *all* the earth. And he has forbidden us to eat swine.

SERGIS: Now look, son! This pig brain is all we've got to eat. It's all the master left us when he butchered yesterday. What are you going to eat—the dried pods those beasties are fighting over up there in the big pen on the hill? *(points to the hill over the heads of the audience)*

OBED: I wish I could!

ANTIPAS: *(alarmed)* Don't try it, Obed! When they get hungry, they will eat anything. The boars are really scary.

SERGIS: *(respectfully)* Let's face it—if we fell down in their midst, those pigs would eat us! The fact that we feed them means nothing. *(to Obed)* Come on Obed, just try a bit of the pig brain.

OBED: In my father's house there is bread enough *and* to spare.

SERGIS: You are always giving us this great story about "in my father's house." If it was such a great place, why did you leave it in the first place?

OBED: *(wistfully)* I wish I knew!

SERGIS: Well, if it's so great, why don't you go home?

OBED: *(sorrowfully)* I wish I could!

SERGIS: Oh, I get a headache talking to you. You won't even call the real name of your God.

You won't eat perfectly good food here and won't go home to where you can get something you will eat. You keep talking about this great house of yours and don't even know why you left it or why you can't go back.

I'm going down to that shady tree by the spring and try to sleep off the rest of the day. Antipas! Watch the pigs! They could break down the the fence and all wander off and our Galilean "prince" here wouldn't even notice.

ANTIPAS: Yes, Father.

SERGIS: *(exits singing the following ditty to the tune of "Jimmy Crack*

Corn")

I wandered off to a willow tree;
I found a lass and she found me;
We sang and we played
And then there were three
underneath the willow tree.

ANTIPAS: I hope you are not angry with my father, Obed.

OBED: No, Antipas, I don't get angry anymore. I have been mocked and taunted so often these past months that I'm used to it . . . sort of . . .

ANTIPAS: My father doesn't mean to be taunting you.

OBED: I know he doesn't, Antipas.

ANTIPAS: *(sees a movement among the pigs on the hill, jumps to his feet, picks up a stone, runs down left with stone in hand, and calls the pigs by rolling a long "r")* Rrrrrrrrrr! quit rooting under that fence post, you with the tusks, or I'll crack your skull. Rrrrrrrrrrrrrr! That's better! Rrrrrrrrrr! That's it. Rrrrrr! *(stops)* Obed, why did you leave home?

OBED: I couldn't stand my brother, I guess, and I thought I didn't need my father.

ANTIPAS: We were all very impressed when you first hit town. They were even talking about it down in Antioch—all about the rich Galilean prince with his beautiful horse and endless supply of gold. Why, last summer you threw away more gold in one night than we make in a year.

OBED: Was it just last summer? It seems like years since I heard my father describe the sunrise around the breakfast table! He was always out before dawn.

ANTIPAS: He must have been a great man!

OBED: He *is* a great man!

ANTIPAS: So, why did you leave him!

OBED: I thought I didn't need him. I guess at one point I didn't even care if he was alive or not. *(remembering)* "Give me my share."

(with bitter disillusionment) I got it all right—all of it!

ANTIPAS: What do you mean?

OBED: *(intensely)* When I was with him, the whole world was mine. *(jumps up)* The whole world! The sky—the valley—the land—the friendly faces in the village—the creaking of the sledges on the threshing floor—the deep laughter of men in the gate—the stately pace of our great camels—the solemn sound of prayer in God's house—our family home. All this was mine—mine with him!

ANTIPAS: And then?

OBED: I threw it all away! I thought I would be free.

ANTIPAS: Weren't you?

OBED: *(laughs bitterly)* Sure I was! Like a severed hand—free from the body.

Like an uprooted plant free from the soil. Like an oar that slips from the rower's hand—free to drift in the sea. It is surrounded by movement, sunlight and sparkling water. The oar thinks it is free, but actually it drifts and rots in the sea. Finally the waves tire of playing with it and cast it up on the shore. A wanderer finds it, breaks it and burns it.

That's what I am, Antipas, broken . . . rotting . . . drying in the sun waiting to be burned.

ANTIPAS: Well, why don't you go home?

OBED: I wish I could!

ANTIPAS: Look, Obed! If you won't eat swine's flesh, you'll starve. I know you think it's wrong, but at least it keeps us alive. Another few days and you'll be too weak to go anywhere!

OBED: I've thought of that.

ANTIPAS: Then you had better start home before it's too late. What's keeping you?

OBED: Three things: my father, my brother, and the village.

ANTIPAS: What do you mean?

OBED:	When I asked for my share, my father gave it to me. He didn't say anything. He just gave me the deeds to a third of the family property. If he had scolded me, I would have answered him and felt better. But he gave them to me without a word.
ANTIPAS:	What then?
OBED:	I had to sell everything quickly because the village was so mad at me. When I found buyers, I took the money and left the village. Now I have lost it all. How can I face him?
ANTIPAS:	What does your brother have to do with it?
OBED:	We hate each other. But it's more than that. When I asked for my share, father divided the property between us. I got mine, he got his. Now mine's gone. If I go back, I will be living off of his portion and be eating his bread. I don't even want to think about how he will treat me.
ANTIPAS:	But Obed! Why do you make it so hard?
OBED:	What do you mean?
ANTIPAS:	Look! Who are you working for now?
OBED:	The house of Abu-Shem.
ANTIPAS:	What do you think of his sons? You know . . . those two fellows who ride by on their sleek, black horses. You remember them! My sister has to hide in the empty grain bin until they are gone!
OBED:	You mean those men who whip us if we don't bow down from the waist as they ride by?
ANTIPAS:	They're the ones. They rode past about two weeks ago.
OBED:	So those are old man Abu-Shem's sons? Yes, that figures!
ANTIPAS:	They are really mean. When any one of the house servants does anything they don't like, they bring his wife and tie her up in a sack and bullwhip her until blood shows through the sack. The servant has to stand and watch it . . .
OBED:	*(knowingly)* . . . and listen to her scream!
ANTIPAS:	You get the picture! But we're hired servants. We have a skill— we can handle pigs. So we don't live in the house or even live

in the village around it. We hardly ever even see those fellows!

OBED: *So?*

ANTIPAS: Look! You're working as a hired man here, and you're starving. Work as a hired man in your own district, and you will at least eat.

OBED: I never thought of that.

ANTIPAS: All you need is job training? Could you do carpentry work or learn to be a stone mason?

OBED: I suppose I could . . . that is, I could if someone would train me.

ANTIPAS: Can you manage that somehow?

OBED: Not *now*. After taking my inheritance and losing it, no one will think I am worth training.

ANTIPAS: What if your father backed you?

OBED: Why should he back me after all that I have done to him?

ANTIPAS: Listen, Obed. You don't have any good options. Would you rather stay here and starve to death?

OBED: The craftsmen who work on our estate make good money.

ANTIPAS: There's your answer—you have to find a way to join them. Can't you make a nice speech to your father and talk him into recommending you for job training just this once.

OBED: I don't know . . . it wouldn't be easy.

ANTIPAS: Look mate, we are in the middle of a famine. Nothing is easy. You had better give it a try. You know . . . dream up a good speech, butter up the old man somehow. Give it a try. You know . . . tell him what he wants to hear!

OBED: *(with a flicker of hope)* What he wants to hear . . . I never thought of that . . . You know Antipas, it just might work. Bread enough *and* to spare—that's the life of the independent craftsmen that work on our estate.

ANTIPAS: That's it, Obed. If that's true, then you could gradually save your money and one day you could pay back what you lost. Then you could be restored as a son to your father's house. Wouldn't that work?

OBED: You know, Antipas . . . it just might. It's a long shot but . . . it just might work! *(remembering)* The last meal in my father's house . . . we left the bread on the table . . . unbroken!

ANTIPAS: Could you get your training in a nearby village?

OBED: It would have to be in another village. There is no way I could live in our village now . . . impossible.

ANTIPAS: Then it's all very simple!

OBED: Of course, it would take me a hundred years to pay it all back, but after a year or two, Father might forgive the rest.

ANTIPAS: At least you'll eat.

OBED: Let's see! What will I tell him? I've got an idea. Once down in Egypt, Pharaoh wanted to butter up Moses, and Pharaoh said to him something like, "I have sinned before heaven and in your sight."

ANTIPAS: That's a fantastic start. Go on . . .

OBED: *(kneels in center of stage and addresses his father in imagination before him—overacts in a dramatic fashion)* "Father, I have sinned against heaven and before you. I am no longer worthy to be called your son. Fashion out of me a craftsman."

ANTIPAS: *(clapping)* Great! That sounds great. You will win the approval of your father. He'll send you off for job training. You won't have to live with your brother, and you will have something to eat.

OBED: It just might work. When can I start?

ANTIPAS: Give me that coin you said you had sewn into the edge of your robe. I'll buy some dried beans and a water skin for you in the village tonight, and before dawn you can be on your way. Take the road by the coast. It's better traveled, and you might even get a ride on a cart. When you hear your own language, head inland and you'll be in Galilee. *(notices that Obed isn't listening)* Are you listening, Obed? *(no answer)* Obed, what's the matter?

OBED: The village!

ANTIPAS: What about the village?

OBED: Remember I told you there were three reasons why I couldn't go home?

ANTIPAS: Yes.

OBED: Well . . . the third one was the village!

ANTIPAS: So what's the problem?

OBED: Think about it, and you'll figure it out! As soon as I am identified at the edge of the village a crowd will begin to gather. First ten, then twenty, soon fifty or more people will surround me and start chanting and clapping. *(walks in a circle around the stage, chanting and clapping; emphasizes in each case the word* idiot *and the word* here *in the following refrain)*
              The *idiot* is *here,* he's *here,* he's *here.*
              The *idiot* is *here,* he's *here! (With greater intensity)*
              The *idiot* is *here,* he's *here,* he's *here.*
              The *idiot* is *here,* he's *here!*
              Then will come the taunts, mixed with thrown chunks of dried manure and garbage.

ANTIPAS: So what is that all about?

OBED: We have a custom in our country. If someone like me loses the family inheritance among people like you Greeks and dares go back to the village, they are really rough on him.

ANTIPAS: Go on.

OBED: They drag him to the middle of town and they break a big clay pot in front of everyone as they chant, "So-and-so is cut off from his people." After that you are finished in that village—no one will talk to you or have anything to do with you.

ANTIPAS: I've heard of stuff like that back in Macedonia, but here we can pick our friends.

OBED: I don't think I can face it!

ANTIPAS: *(angry and shouting)* All right—go ahead and starve to death. What do I care?

(pause) Take your choice, Obed!

OBED: You're right, Antipas. I don't have any choice.

ANTIPAS: Besides, you got yourself into this mess didn't you?

OBED: Yeah—I did! It's all my fault!

ANTIPAS: Well, you had better brace up and take it like a man.

OBED: I don't know if I can. *(looks up the hill in front of him)* If only I were a pig and could eat pods.

ANTIPAS: Well, you aren't and you can't. Come on, let's have that coin.

OBED: *(tearing off a piece of the hem of his robe and passing it to Antipas)* It's gold. Be sure and get as much as you can. I have a long and bitter road to travel.

ANTIPAS: *(starting out)* I'll do my best. Watch the pigs until I get back, Obed. *(exits)*

OBED: Don't worry, the pen is strong enough. They can't go anywhere. *(starts to pantomime the actions of the expected crowd in the village; stands spread-eagled and pantomimes laughter; then points to the imagined beggar and swings his foot in a swift kick; laughs and points again; reaches up to tear the imagined beggar's garment. Then he pantomimes picking up a large pot, raising it over his head and throwing it on the ground. Suddenly he stops, freezes and covers his face with his hands as he remembers that he is the beggar. He sinks to his knees and then collapses on the ground and cries.)* Oh, Adonai!

Lights dim out.

Scene Three

The Robe

After betrayal and estrangement, the two are now on a journey toward reconciliation. There are five sets of parallel letters in the Arabic words on the two lines in the plate. Father and son come together because the father "ran and fell upon his neck and kissed him."

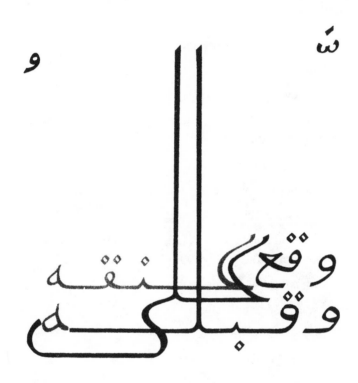

He Fell upon His Neck
and Kissed Him

Scene Three

Time: A month later. About 4:00 in the afternoon.

Place: The same room as scene one. *(As the lights come up, Obed is seated on a chair pulled out from the dining table in his father's house. He is dressed in a clean, white, long-flowing robe. Shaluk is going through a closet at the back of the room. A large loaf of bread lies on the center of the table.)*

SHALUK:	How does it feel to be clean?
OBED:	Unnatural!
SHALUK:	I believe you! Do those sandals fit?
OBED:	I can't even feel them. The calluses on my feet must be a quarter of an inch thick by now.
SHALUK:	You'll get used to them.
OBED:	That herd of pigs seems a million miles away.
SHALUK:	*(surprised)* That herd of what?
OBED:	Pigs! You know, Shaluk, pigs. The animals with the short tusks that root in the ground. I ended up feeding pigs.
SHALUK:	*(amazed)* I would never have believed it!
OBED:	I was desperate, Shaluk.
SHALUK:	I guess you were!
OBED:	A man doesn't give up his pride easily.
SHALUK:	Here—put on this signet ring.
OBED:	Shaluk, I'm almost scared to. Adam will really be mad about this!
SHALUK:	Your father trusts you now.
OBED:	But Shaluk . . . this ring will give me authority Adam won't want me to have.
SHALUK:	Your father is the head of the house, not Adam. Go ahead . . . put it on!
OBED:	*(putting it on)* How can I ever use it?

SHALUK: You may never have to. It is a statement your father wants to make. And every time you look at it just repeat to yourself, "I am unworthy."

OBED: Don't worry! I will. I will.

SHALUK: *(bringing a gorgeous outer robe from the closet)* Now, try this robe on for length.

OBED: But Shaluk! That's Father's robe!

SHALUK: *(quietly)* You don't think there's anything around here that belongs to *you* anymore, do you?

OBED: *(quietly)* I guess not.

SHALUK: You took your portion—remember?

OBED: I remember.

SHALUK: Well?

OBED: But that's the robe Father wears on feast days!

SHALUK: He told me to dress you in the "best robe," didn't he?

OBED: I didn't hear a thing.

SHALUK: I expect not. *(laying the robe over the back of a chair)*

OBED: All I can remember is seeing Father with the front edge of his garment in his hand running down the street, with all the kids in the street running after him—laughing.

SHALUK: I know. I was there.

OBED: *(astounded)* He embraced me . . . me! With all of my filth and lice and rags.

SHALUK: You were pretty dirty!

OBED: And the tears streaming down his face . . . I'll never forget it!

SHALUK: I hope you don't.

OBED: I didn't think it would be like that at all.

SHALUK: That's because you never knew until that moment what your father was really like.

OBED: I still don't!

SHALUK: Yes, but now you have a chance to learn.

OBED: I thought all the people of the village would be running after me.

SHALUK: They would have been.

OBED: I knew what it would be like: the curses, the taunts, the stones, the mockery, the breaking of the great pot. I had it all figured out.

SHALUK: So did he!

OBED: I guess he did. You know, when I started home . . . I still didn't get it! The only reason I came home was because I was hungry. I thought that my only hope was to learn a trade, get a job and pay the money back.

SHALUK: *(in amazement)* After what . . . a hundred years? I can't believe it!

OBED: You heard the first part of my speech which was "I have sinned before heaven and in your sight and am no longer worthy to be called your son."

SHALUK: And the end?

OBED: I was going to close with "Fashion out of me a craftsman." I carefully rehearsed the whole thing.

SHALUK: And then you couldn't say the last line.

OBED: That's right. One look in his face, and all I could do was admit that I was wrong and blurt out, "I am unworthy to be called your son."

SHALUK: *(picks up the loaf on the table)* What's this, Obed?

OBED: A loaf of our family's bread. Why?

SHALUK: Every day since you left I have put a fresh, unbroken loaf on the table. It was not eaten. Then at night I threw it away. In the morning I put another in its place. It was your father's order.

OBED: I don't get it.

SHALUK: He would come in each morning, look at it, and say quietly,

"The bread is unbroken."

OBED: What did he mean?

SHALUK: He said that when he had sons in restored fellowship with him, he would break bread with them. Until that happened, the bread would lie unbroken.

OBED: But Adam was here!

SHALUK: *(sadly)* Adam has not changed.

OBED: *(knowingly)* I see.

SHALUK: Each day the loaf sat there unbroken.

OBED: And each day his heart broke a little more. I never understood.

SHALUK: Until today! I tried to tell you that night!

OBED: I wasn't listening!

SHALUK: All I got out of you was, "Give me my share." Remember?

OBED: I remember. The only share that matters now is a portion of the broken bread of Father's fellowship.

SHALUK: *(earnestly)* Your father broke *himself* this afternoon on the road before the village.

OBED: I know.

SHALUK: *(holding up the robe)* But here! Put this robe on. Come on now! I have my orders.

OBED: *(stands and slowly puts on the robe Shaluk is holding for him)* My father's robe. I . . . I . . . I don't know what to say.

SHALUK: *(firmly)* Don't say anything. Just remember that the only thing you brought back to this house was a handful of filthy rags.

OBED: I'll not forget. *(sits)* You know, Shaluk, I never thought about it, but actually I was demanding that Father fulfill my condition.

SHALUK: What was that?

OBED: That I would come home only if he drove Adam out.

SHALUK: He loves Adam too, you know!

OBED: I'm sure he does, but I don't know how!

SHALUK: *(exploding)* What do you mean you don't know how? Was it so easy for him to love you?

OBED: Sorry, Shaluk. You're right; of course, it wasn't! I didn't really mean that.

SHALUK: He doesn't love you because you're lovely—remember the rags!

OBED: I remember.

SHALUK: He loves both of you because that's the kind of person he is, and he knows how desperately you need his love. But you never understood until you saw him get hurt for you!

OBED: I guess that's why he had to do it. *(pause)* You know, Shaluk, I thought the only thing between us was the money.

SHALUK: *(startled)* The money!

OBED: I know it sounds pretty ridiculous. A month ago it seemed so right.

SHALUK: You were really in a far country. Break his heart . . . and offer him a denarius. Reject his love . . . and pay him silver. Long for his death and transfer a bank account. What better way to rub salt into a wound!

OBED: I know, I know.

SHALUK: Then we would have had two Adams in this house.

OBED: Yeah—I would have turned into another Adam.

SHALUK: Well, when your brother comes in from the fields at sundown, just remember all of this, will you?

OBED: I'll remember. We have each rejected our father's love only in different ways. I have done it while breaking the law. Adam does it while keeping the law.

SHALUK: *(meaningfully)* Well done. That pretty much summarizes where the two of you have been for years.

FATHER: *(calling from outside)* Obed! Obed!

SHALUK: He is ready, Abu-Adam. *(Father enters; Obed stands)*

FATHER: *(seeing Obed in the new robe)* Good—very good! I like your selection, Shaluk.

SHALUK: It was the best one, Abu-Adam.

OBED: Father, I . . . I . . . I'm unworthy!

FATHER: We have already heard that today, son.

OBED: Yes, I know.

FATHER: From now on just say it to yourself. You look good, son, really good! You have no idea what it means to have the wall between us demolished—at long last! Shaluk! Set the table for two guests. Both the mayor and the priest will be here tonight.

SHALUK: Everything is ready, Abu-Adam. I have even written a song!

FATHER: *(excitedly)* Wonderful! I can hardly wait to hear it!

OBED: Father?

FATHER: Yes, son?

OBED: Father . . . I . . . it's always meant so much to me . . . will you break the bread tonight?

FATHER: *(going to the table and picking up the loaf and saying very slowly)* Tonight . . . yes . . . tonight . . . tonight I will break the bread.

The lights dim.

Scene Four

The Banquet

Tragically, the father's final speech is in defense of joy. The prodigal's entire spiritual pilgrimage is pictured in this plate. There is resurrection. He was *dead* and is *alive*. There is restoration. He was *lost* and is *found*. The older son needs to move through the same pilgrimage—but will he be willing?

This One Was Dead and Is Alive
Was Lost and Is Found

Scene Four

Time: A few hours later, about sundown.

Place: The same as scene three only the table is to one side with four chairs arranged like a sitting room.

As the scene opens, Shaluk is busy dusting the room, spreading a tablecloth on the table, putting glasses on the table, arranging the chairs and placing a plate with one loaf of bread on it on the table. He sings as he works.

(music on page 148)

SHALUK:	*(singing)* On this happy day, Obed has been found, Here is where he'll stay, Joy cannot be bound. Chorus Let all join in song To show forth our joy, For he has been found, Obed, precious boy.

continues humming the same tune

OBED:	*(entering excitedly)* Are they here yet?
SHALUK:	No, they're not here. Relax, won't you?
OBED:	Relax! How can I? What about Adam? Has he come in from the fields?
SHALUK:	Not yet.
OBED:	He must be staying away.
SHALUK:	Easy there, Obed, easy! He's not staying away. This morning he said he was going to take a crew of men and repair the terraces in the olive orchard on the east slope. We tried to get word to him but couldn't find him. He hasn't even heard you're home! He'll be in. Don't worry.
OBED:	I just wish it were over.
SHALUK:	Now look, Obed! What your father did this afternoon restored

you to the whole village, not just to our house. That was part of his plan. The mayor is obliged to welcome you. As to the priest . . . well . . . you know he is a kindly old gentleman. He's always been your friend.

OBED: *(only somewhat reassured)* I suppose you are right.

FATHER: *(entering from stage right)* Shaluk! Is everything ready?

SHALUK: All is ready, Abu-Adam.

FATHER: What about the meat? Is it cooked?

SHALUK: It will be ready in half an hour. And there will be plenty for all of us.

FATHER: *(sees the table and the chairs)* Yes, that's right—the four of us will chat and eat a bit here first. Then we'll join the crowd in the banquet hall. You can start serving when Adam arrives. He will help serve, as usual, to show honor to our guests.

OBED: But, Father, I can't sit with you!

FATHER: Nonsense! You must! I have to make very sure that the mayor and the priest know that I have accepted you. They will follow suit. The rest of the crowd will take their clue from the two of them. *(a loud, firm knock on the door stage right)* Shaluk! The door!

Shaluk crosses and opens the door. The mayor and the priest enter in that order. The father greets them first.

MAYOR: *(shaking hands with the father)* Congratulations, Abu-Adam, on the reconciliation you have achieved with your son.

FATHER: *(greeting them with a very enthusiastic handclasp)* Thank you, Your Honor. Welcome, Abuna—it is good of you to come.

PRIEST: Yes . . . well . . . you need to know that we are here because we respect you and honor what you have done.

MAYOR: *(to Obed)* You don't need to hide, Obed. You heard Abuna. We are here to rejoice with your father. And keep in mind—if your father accepts you—then we accept you even though you have a ways yet to go. Do you understand?

OBED: I do, Your Honor, and I won't let you down again.

PRIEST: Obed!

They embrace.

OBED: Abuna! All the time I was gone, the sound of your voice read-
               ing the Psalms was ringing in my ears.

PRIEST: *(with a smile)* I don't know how that could be true. You never
               listened in the synagogue when you were here.

All laugh.

OBED: From now on I'll be listening. Trust me.

ABUNA: *(with a pat on Obed's shoulder)* I do and I will.

OBED: Thank you, Abuna.

FATHER: I am delighted that you have come, Abuna. I know that you
               have a service later tonight. We have burdened you.

PRIEST: Not at all, Abu-Adam, I am honored to be here. This is an
               amazing day in the village.

MAYOR: *(solemnly)* No other father in the village would have been will-
               ing to do what you have done today. We have never seen such
               things. Come sit with us, my boy!

OBED: I can't, O Mayor!

MAYOR: What do you mean you can't! *(gets up, goes over to Obed and
               drags him over to the empty chair)* Of course you can. I am
               asking you to sit with us for one reason—the robe that you are
               wearing.

OBED: I understand, Your Honor.

FATHER: Shaluk, bring some hot tea for the guests.

SHALUK: *(has been standing respectfully at the back of the room)* Yes,
               Sir. *(goes to the back of the room and pours four glasses and
               serves them during the following speeches)*

FATHER: And then let's have your new song.

MAYOR: Wonderful idea! By all means, let's hear it. You're the best bal-
               lad singer in the village, Shaluk. No banquet would be com-

plete without one of your songs.

SHALUK: *(apologetically)* Really, we've been so busy. I've had only to-day. It isn't much. *(By this time he has served a small glass of tea to the four from a tray.)*

PRIEST: Nonsense! Let's hear it!

SHALUK: *(sings a capella or accompanies himself on mandolin, guitar or drum)*[1]
On this happy day,
Obed has been found.
Here is where he'll stay;
Joy cannot be bound.

Chorus

Let all join in song
To show forth our joy,
For he has been found.
Obed, precious boy.

Tonight let us feast
On the fatted calf;
Our sorrow has ceased;
Now's the time to laugh.

Chorus (repeated)

(On the chorus of the second verse, Shaluk waves his hands for them all to join. They sing the chorus with him in each succeeding time around, clapping in rhythm as they sing.)

Our Mayor is here,
Brilliant as the light;
So gone is our fear;
He defends our right.

Chorus (in unison)

MAYOR: *(clapping and very pleased)* Well done—well done! Didn't I tell you Shaluk was the best ballad singer in the village? Let's

---

[1]The music for this song is on page 148.

have a verse on Abuna here.

SHALUK: Patience, Your Honor. *(sings)*

The priest brings us cheer;
Blessed is his face;
With him ever near,
Forgot is disgrace.

Chorus *(all join in)*

PRIEST: I might even let you visit your friends on the sabbath for that, Shaluk.

They all laugh good-naturedly.

MAYOR: I know you're not finished, Shaluk. Let's have the last verse.

SHALUK: *(sings)*
The father is here,
Elder to us all.
His love brings us near,
Let us heed his call.

Chorus *(all join in)*

During the singing of this last chorus Adam comes down the aisle and stands on the lower level at a distance. As the song finishes, there is much clapping and sounds all around of "wonderful," "best ballad we have heard in years," "we'll have to learn that one," etc. Adam breaks in harshly.

ADAM: What's going on here? What is all this noise? Why have I not been consulted? *(calling in a louder voice)* Shaluk! Shaluk!

FATHER: *(turning to Shaluk)* Shaluk, go out and speak to him. Tell him the story of the reconciliation I have achieved. Inform him that his father and his father's guests await him. You know . . . explain everything.

SHALUK: Yes, sir. *(exits to the lower level)*

MAYOR: *(leaning over to the father in a stage whisper)* What's the matter with Adam?

FATHER: *(reflecting sadly)* He always talks that way.

OBED: Would you rather I left, Father?

FATHER: Stay where you are, son.

ADAM: *(out in the garden or on the lower level—angrily)* What's the story, Shaluk? What's going on? It seems there is a banquet. Why have I not been consulted?

SHALUK: We did our best to reach you but could not find you. Yes, there is a banquet tonight. *(solemnly)* Adam, this morning your brother appeared unexpectedly at the edge of the village.

ADAM: *(slowly, with incredulity, trying to absorb this new and rather frightening fact)* My . . . brother! Who do you mean?

SHALUK: Your brother—Obed!

ADAM: *(stunned)* Obed! I see. *(slowly and anxiously)* And . . . ah . . . how many retainers did he have with him? Who paid for this banquet?

SHALUK: He appeared alone—barefoot and in rags.

ADAM: *(relieved)* I see! *(after a brief pause for reflection, he continues impatiently)* Then what happened? I presume that the village expressed appropriate displeasure at his condition and what it signifies. Come on—out with it! I'm in a hurry? I have yet to bathe and dress for the evening service.

SHALUK: The village spotted him and was ready to respond as you put it, "appropriately." But your father saw him at a great distance, for he was watching from the balcony. He hurried down, took the edge of his robe in hand and ran through the village down the road. Half the village ran after him. Then he fell on your brother's neck and kissed him right in front of all of us. *(pause)* Are you listening to me, Adam?

ADAM: Of course I'm listening! But I don't believe you. My father is an honorable man. He wouldn't do such a thing. Now tell me the truth or you will regret it. *(raises his stick very slightly to signal a veiled threat)*

SHALUK: *(unbowed)* As always, I am telling you the truth, Adam. And not only that, but Obed accepted your father's love, confessed his sin and his unworthiness. Then your father ordered us to dress your brother in the best robe and put shoes on his feet and the ring on his finger. He then announced to the village that he had found his son and brought him back from death to life. Finally he ordered a banquet to celebrate the fact that he had found and resurrected his lost, dead son. We entered the village in a kind of a parade.

ADAM: *(with anger and apprehension)* So he is now wearing the signet ring of the house.

SHALUK: He is indeed.

ADAM: Ridiculous! With that ring Obed will probably try to sell my share the same way he sold his own. He took his portion! Why should he come here and expect to live off of mine?

SHALUK: Your father trusts him, Adam.

ADAM: How could he after what's happened?

SHALUK: We killed the fatted calf to celebrate the peace your father has achieved at great cost.

ADAM: *(not listening)* One day that calf would have been mine, you know. Everything left in this house will be mine by right!

SHALUK: I repeat, the banquet is a celebration of the success of your father's efforts in finding and reviving your brother The mayor and the priest have arrived. They are waiting in the reception room for you. Your father wants you to come and greet his guests and help serve the banquet. We have orders to start when you are ready.

FATHER: *(from inside the room, turning to the mayor)* Listen! You will see what he is like!

MAYOR: What do you mean?

PRIEST: Shhh!

ADAM: *(deliberates briefly, then makes the big decision and says firmly)* I had hoped to present my views before Father decided what to do with this worthless boy. Obed should be driven from the village until he returns the money. But it seems that Father has offered peace without asking Obed to do anything.

SHALUK: Indeed he has. I witnessed it, and it was stunning!

ADAM: I will not enter that house!

Obed jumps up and starts to rush out. The father stands up and grabs him.

FATHER: No, Obed! *(gently but firmly pushes Obed back into his seat)* You can do nothing.

SHALUK: Adam! This is unacceptable. You must at least enter the banquet hall and greet your father's guests. You know the customs.

ADAM: So you want me to join in a banquet with an unclean, polluted beggar.

SHALUK: Such honorable thoughts!

ADAM: Someone has to care for honor in this house!

SHALUK: *(sharply)* Adam! Don't insult your father in his own house before these distinguished guests. I repeat—you must at least go in and greet them. After that you can pretend that you are not feeling well and withdraw. But you must greet them.

ADAM: *(firmly)* It has been a struggle to uphold our family's honor ever since that beggar left. Now father has made a hero out of him!

SHALUK: *(very firmly)* No Adam, your father has not made a hero out of your brother, he has created a son. In the process he has shown himself to be a prince.

ADAM: *(not listening)* Now listen, Shaluk. Some things are pretty basic. One of them is . . . you get what you pay for. But this beggar has been restored to the family without paying a single denarius. I want no part of this. I won't go in! That's final! *(pauses)* I said that's final! *(goes through the arch and sits out of sight behind the wall)*

SHALUK: *(sadly admitting defeat)* You're the older son. *(he goes in; slowly, reluctantly he says)* Abu-Adam, may I have a word with you!

FATHER: We heard everything from the window, Shaluk. The story is clear. Adam won't come in. What do you think we should do?

SHALUK: I don't know. *(in deep sadness)* I really don't know.

FATHER: Very well, hold up the banquet until I give the word.

SHALUK: Very well, sir. *(starts out, pauses at the door)* I am sorry, Abu-Adam.

FATHER: We have been through this before, haven't we, Shaluk?

SHALUK: *(sadly)* Yes . . . we have. *(exits)*

OBED: *(jumps up, pleading)* Father! Let me go out and talk to him.

FATHER: That would just make matters worse, son. We have enough hostility to deal with. We don't need more.

OBED: *(sits down)* Very well, Father.

MAYOR: But why he is so angry, Abu-Adam?

FATHER: *(thoughtfully)* He is mad because of my unconditional love for his brother.

PRIEST: Is this not the same kind of love you daily extend to him?

FATHER: It is . . . but Adam has yet to see it.

MAYOR: Gentlemen, things are fairly straightforward to me. A family, like a village, must have order. You, the father, requested his presence at this banquet. He has refused. There must be consequences to such a public insult!

FATHER: It is very complicated, Your Honor. He thinks he is the ideal son protecting the honor of the house. To do that he feels he must oppose the reconciliation I have made with his brother.

MAYOR: This kind of insolence cannot be ignored. I am a mayor! I understand these things! Your authority over him must be asserted.

FATHER: I share your concern, Your Honor. Officially and formally he does what I tell him, which I appreciate. But there is always that edge. He thinks he knows better than I how to preserve the honor of this house.

MAYOR: But he doesn't and must be punished for his arrogance. Lock him up, refuse to see him, make him eat in the barn . . . as a last resort, thrash him!

PRIEST: But, Your Honor, this is not a servant; it is a son. Abu-Adam is not his master; he is his father.

FATHER: Your Honor, it's hard to beat a man into loving you! What you propose is a good solution for a troublesome servant. It is not good enough for a son. Punishment will only bring anger and resentment.

PRIEST: *(addressing the mayor)* This is not like the problems you meet in the gate, Your Honor.

OBED: It would not have worked with me.

MAYOR: Can you set up strict rules for him to follow?

FATHER: More rules will increase his pride that he has kept them.

MAYOR: *(gives in)* Yes, I see your point.

FATHER: I don't want a fearful servant, I long for a loving son.

PRIEST: If that's the case, Abu-Adam, you need to love and forgive.

FATHER: Always I have loved. Many times I have forgiven. But now he is a man, and this is no longer enough.

PRIEST: How's that?

FATHER: *(earnestly)* Because he will not accept. He will answer, "Forgiven for what? I have done nothing. I ask only for my rights."

OBED: "Give me my share." This is all so agonizingly familiar.

MAYOR: *(turning to the priest)* Abuna, the boy must not be allowed to insult his father in public in this outrageous manner.

PRIEST: *(glaring at the mayor and then turning to the father)* You must show him love, Abu-Adam.

FATHER: Abuna, authentic love is never a sign of weakness. It is sign of great strength. But do you really want me to ignore this public insult and say, "Go ahead, insult me any time you like"?

MAYOR: Never! This is weakness, not love.

PRIEST: *(backing down)* Yes, I see what you mean.

OBED: Abuna, Father demonstrates love every day in this home. But I never understood it until this afternoon.

PRIEST: *(quietly)* Yes. We heard all about it.

FATHER: Abuna, I am ready to forgive. But I must offer forgiveness in a way that has hope of changing him. I want to restore our fellowship.

PRIEST: Yes, of course!

FATHER: Forgiveness is not just letting the man who has done wrong go free.

PRIEST: What is it then?

FATHER: Forgiveness opens the door for a return of fellowship. Your Honor!

MAYOR: Yes, Abu-Adam.

FATHER: What if a gang of thieves attacks our village; we fight them; and then, in the middle of the fight, you as mayor cry out and say to them, "I forgive you."

MAYOR: Ridiculous!

FATHER: Why?

MAYOR: It would change nothing. The fight would continue as before.

FATHER: Abuna, forgiveness is not complete until it heals the broken relationship.

MAYOR: I insist! The honor of the house must be preserved by discipline.

PRIEST: But, Your Honor, he must show love!

MAYOR: *(standing)* But, Abuna, without discipline and order all honor is lost.

PRIEST: *(right to his face)* This is not a servant! This is his son! The Scriptures say, "He does not deal with us according to our sins."

MAYOR: *(delighted to be able to top him)* But Abuna! The Scriptures also say, "Let justice roll down like waters, and righteousness like an ever-flowing stream."

Both now shouting ad lib at once.

FATHER: *(jumping up to separate them)* Don't be angry, my friends. Don't be angry. You are both right, dead right. The fire has both light and heat. My son needs both love and discipline. But neither one alone will solve anything.

MAYOR: *(calms down)* What will you do then?

FATHER: *(goes slowly up to the table, picks up a loaf, slowly breaks it and lays it back down)* I will humble myself before the community and go out to him.

MAYOR: That's a risky thing to do. He is unstable. We can't predict his response.

FATHER: *(softly)* I know.

MAYOR: *(firmly)* That settles it. Then you mustn't go.

FATHER: *(with intensity and exasperation)* Discipline will bring more rebellion. Forgiveness will change nothing. What is it you want me to do? *(both are silent, and the father continues quietly)* Only costly love can change the hardened heart.

MAYOR: Abu-Adam, we don't want you to get hurt.

FATHER: I am already hurt! Can't you understand? I go, my friends.

Priest and mayor rise to forcibly stop him from going out.

OBED: *(standing up)* Father, I . . .

FATHER: Perhaps you can explain it to them, Obed.

OBED: *(collapses in his chair, buries his face in his hands)* O Father!

FATHER: *(commanding and pushing them back with his arm)* Do not interfere with what I must do.
(goes out and down to lower garden level and continues) My son, my son . . .

ADAM: *(appearing)* What do you want?

FATHER: My son, why are you angry?

ADAM: I'm not angry.

FATHER: Come into the banquet then. We have music and dancing. The mayor is here and Abuna, the priest. They ask for you. Your brother, is here. He wants to see you.

ADAM: I won't go in.

FATHER: Why, my son?

ADAM: I'm not getting my rights. I'm not being treated fairly.

FATHER: What do you mean, son?

ADAM: Lo, these many years I have served you, and I never disobeyed your command; yet you never gave me a kid that I might make merry with my friends. But when this son of yours came, who has devoured your living with harlots, you killed for him the fatted calf!

FATHER: *(firmly)* My son! You've just come from the fields and have heard nothing. We don't yet know how he lost his money.

ADAM: I don't need reports. I know what he is like.

FATHER: Yes, and I understand both of you. But this banquet is not in honor of your brother. I have found my son and brought him to life. These good friends are celebrating with me. They have come to honor me, not your brother. Will you not join us?

ADAM: He is a dog that has come to eat up my share of the inheritance.

FATHER: Son, you are always with me, and all that is mine is yours. It was fitting to make merry and be glad, for this your brother was dead and is alive; he was lost and is found.

ADAM: He is not my brother. He is a dirty beggar. Now I must share my portion with a beggar. Maybe if I ran away and spent the family's money on prostitutes, then you would love me.

FATHER: Still, I would love you. Adam, I understand that you want me to refuse the company of sinners.

ADAM: Indeed I do.

FATHER: But, son, if I do that . . . I will have to avoid you.

ADAM: *(very angry)* There is no way I can understand what you are saying. He ruins everything and gets a banquet. I try to hold things together and get nothing! Something has to give around here! *(stands for a moment, raises his stick slightly, gripping it with both hands and then slowly brings it down)* But right now, I can't waste any more time. I have to change for evening prayers. *(stomps off)*

FATHER: *(gently calling after Adam)* Of course, you mustn't be late to pray! *(he then returns slowly to the stage)*

MAYOR: Abu-Adam, this is a dangerous man who must be dealt with.

FATHER: *(quietly and firmly)* He is my son and I will love him . . . to the end. Abuna!

PRIEST: Yes, Abu-Adam.

FATHER: Adam will be in your congregation tonight.

PRIEST: *(shaking his head)* I know, I know.

FATHER: What are you going to do about him?

PRIEST: About him? About him? What am I going to do about . . . all of us?

MAYOR: Yes, about all of us.

The mayor and the priest put their hands on the father's shoulders.

The lights dim.

Production Notes

In an earlier version scene four has been used as a separate play or play reading for a number of years in Africa and Asia as well as in America. With very little adaptation it can still be used in this fashion.

The stage needs two entrances. Stage right comes in from the street. Stage left leads into the inner quarters of the house. In scene four I suggest that the older son enter through the audience and play his scene on a lower level, down right.

For the father's staff in scene one, use a round, four-foot stick about 1 inch in diameter (broomstick, doweling or natural stick). With a fine saw cut it about three-fourths through, and paint it. Then the father will be able to break it easily over his knee.

If the anticipated audience is not be familiar with Luke 15:11-32, I suggest printing it in the program notes.

Abuna means "our father" and is the appropriate title for a priest. It can be changed to "Father" if desired.

Music for Shaluk's Song

The Cross of Christ

An Egyptian Village Folk Tune

Saleeb al-Maseeh

Bibliography

Works Cited

Arndt, William F., and F. Wilbur Gingrich. *A Greek-English Lexicon of the New Testament and Other Early Christian Literature*. Chicago: University of Chicago Press, 1957.

Ayrout, Henry Habib. *The Fellaheen*. Translated by Hilary Wayment. Rev. ed. Cairo: R. Schindler, 1945.

Bailey, Kenneth E. *Jacob and the Prodigal: How Jesus Retold Israel's Story*. Downers Grove, Ill.: InterVarsity Press, 2003.

———. *Poet and Peasant and Through Peasant Eyes*. Grand Rapids: Eerdmans, 1980.

The Bible in Aramaic. Edited by Alexander Sperber. Vol. 1, *The Pentateuch According to Targum Onkelos*. Leiden: Brill, 1959.

Bishop, Eric F. F. *Jesus of Palestine: The Local Background to the Gospel Documents*. London: Lutterworth, 1955.

Donahue, John R. "Tax Collector." In *Anchor Bible Dictionary*. Vol. 6. Edited by David Noel Freedman. New York: Doubleday, 1992.

Forsyth, P. T. *God the Holy Father*. Naperville, Ill.: Allenson, 1957.

Jeremias, Joachim. *Jerusalem in the Time of Jesus*. Philadelphia: Fortress, 1967.

———. *The Parables of Jesus*. New York: Scribner's, 1963.

Moulton, James Hope, and George Milligan. *The Vocabulary of the Greek Testament Illustrated from the Papyri and Other Non-literary Sources*. Grand Rapids: Eerdmans, 1963.

Robinson, A. T. *A Grammar of the Greek New Testament in the Light of Historical Research*. 4th ed. Nashville: Broadman, 1934.

Salatin, Rudolf Carl von. *Fire and Sword in the Sudan 1879-1895*. London: Edward Arnold, 1907.

Trench, R. C. *Notes on the Parables of Our Lord*. London: John W. Parker, 1857.

Selected Works for Further Study

Bailey, Kenneth E. *Finding the Lost: Cultural Keys to Luke 15.* St. Louis: Concordia, 1992.

Blomberg, Craig L. *Interpreting the Parables.* Downers Grove, Ill.: InterVarsity Press, 1990.

Black, Matthew. *An Aramaic Approach to the Gospels and Acts.* Oxford: Clarendon Press, 1967.

Bornkamm, Günther. *Jesus of Nazareth.* New York: Harper & Row, 1960.

Dalman, Gustaf. *Arbeit und Sitte in Palastina.* 7 vols. Gutersloh: C. Bertelsmann, 1927.

———. *Jesus-Jeshua: Studies in the Gospels.* New York: Ktav, 1971.

———. *The Words of Jesus: Considered in the Light of Post-Biblical Jewish Writings and the Aramaic Language.* Edinburgh: T & T Clark, 1902.

Derrett, J. Duncan M. *Jesus's Audience: The Social and Psychological Environment in Which He Worked.* New York: Seabury Press, 1973.

———. *Law in the New Testament.* London: Darton, Longman & Todd, 1970.

Dodd, C. H. *The Founder of Christianity.* New York: Macmillan, 1970.

———. *The Parables of the Kingdom.* Rev. ed. New York: Scribner's Sons, 1961.

Donahue, John R. *The Gospel in Parable.* Philadelphia: Fortress, 1988.

Edersheim, Alfred. *Sketches of Jewish Social Life in the Days of Christ.* Grand Rapids: Eerdmans, 1974.

Flusser, David. *Jesus.* Jerusalem: Magnes Press, 1997.

Hultgren, Arland J. *The Parables of Jesus.* Grand Rapids: Eerdmans, 2000.

Johnston, Robert M. *Parabolic Interpretations Attributed to Tannaim.* 2 vols. Ph.D. diss., Hartford Seminary Foundation, 1977. Available from UMI Dissertation Services.

Lachs, Samuel T. *A Rabbinic Commentary on the New Testament: The Gospels of Matthew, Mark and Luke.* Hoboken: Ktav, 1987.

Lightfoot, John. *A Commentary on the New Testament from the Talmud and Hebraica.* 4 vols. Grand Rapids: Baker, 1959.

Manson, T. W. *The Teaching of Jesus: Studies of its Form and Content.* Cambridge: Cambridge University Press, 1955.

———. *The Sayings of Jesus: As Recorded in the Gospels According to St. Matthew and St. Luke Arranged with Introduction and Commentary.* London: SCM Press, 1964.

Mishnah, The. Translated by Herbert Danby. Oxford: Oxford University Press, 1980.

Moore, George Foot. *Judaism in the First Centuries of the Christian Era.* 2 vols. New York: Schocken, 1971.

Nouwen, Henri J. M. *The Return of the Prodigal Son.* New York: Doubleday, 1994.

Oesterley, W. O. E. *The Gospel Parables in the Light of their Jewish Background.* London: SPCK, 1936.

Riesenfeld, Harald. *The Gospel Tradition*. Philadelphia: Fortress, 1970.

Rihbany, Abraham M. *The Syrian Christ*. Boston: Houghton Mifflin, 1916.

Safrai, S., and M. Stern, eds. *The Jewish People in the First Century: Historical Geography, Political History, Social, Cultural and Religious Life and Institutions*. 2 vols. Philadelphia: Fortress, 1974, 1976.

Scherer, George H. *The Eastern Colour of the Bible*. London: National Sunday School Union, n.d.

Strack, H. and Billerbeck, P. *Kommentar zum Neuen Testament aus Talmud und Midrash*. 6 vols. Munich: C. H. Beck, 1922-1961.

Wenham, David. *The Parables of Jesus: Pictures of Revolution*. London: Hodder & Stoughton, 1989.

Wright, N. T. *The Challenge of Jesus: Rediscovering Who Jesus Was and Is*. Downers Grove, Ill.: InterVarsity Press, 1999.

———. *Jesus and the Victory of God: Christian Origins and the Question of God*. Vol. 2. Minneapolis: Fortress Press, 1996.

Urbach, Ephraim E. *The Sages: Their Concepts and Beliefs*. 2 vols. Jerusalem: Magnes Press, 1987.